AF264859

Business Cycles and Long Waves: A Behavioral Disequilibrium Perspective

John D. Sterman
and
Erik Mosekilde

WP# 3528-93-MSA   January, 1993

MASSACHUSETTS
INSTITUTE OF TECHNOLOGY
50 MEMORIAL DRIVE
CAMBRIDGE, MASSACHUSETTS 02139

Business Cycles and Long Waves A Behavioral
Disequilibrium Perspective

John D Sterman
and
Erik Mosekilde

WP# 3528-93-MSA   January, 1993

1393

D-4308

Business Cycles and Long Waves:
A Behavioral Disequilibrium
Perspective*

John D Sterman
Sloan School of Management
Massachusetts Institute of Technology
Cambridge, MA 02139 USA

and

Erik Mosekilde
Physics Laboratory III
Technical University of Denmark
2800 Lyngby
Denmark

December 1992

* Forthcoming in Semmler, W (ed) *Business Cycles Theory and Empirical Methods*
Dordrecht: Kluwer Academic Publishers

Please address correspondence to John Sterman at the address above or jsterman@mit edu

This work was supported in part by the Sponsors of the MIT System Dynamics National Model
Project. Jesper Skovhus Thomsen assisted in the preparation of the computer simulations

I Introduction

The evolution of the macroeconomy reflects the interaction of multiple modes of behavior By a
mode of behavior we mean a particular pattern of dynamic behavior, such as growth or fluctuation,
caused by a particular set of feedback processes The most important mode is the long-term exponential growth of the world economy This exponential growth, both cause and consequence of
industrialization, population growth, capital accumulation, technological advance, and historical
accident, has accelerated dramatically since the beginning of the industrial revolution, transforming
virtually every aspect of our world, including economic, political, cultural, and even biogeochemi-
cal systems [1]

Yet economic development around the growth trend is far from steady Indeed, cyclical fluctuations are a persistent feature of economic life Economic historians have identified several distinct
cycles, including the short-term business cycle (3-7 years), the construction or Kuznets cycle (15-
25 years), and the long wave or Kondratieff cycle (40-60 years) The existence of these cycles is
not without controversy, however Debate continues today about the causes of the short-term
business cycle, the most extensively studied mode The causes and even the existence of the
longer cycles are still more controversial In part, the uncertainty is empirical we necessarily have
data for fewer long cycles than short ones. Yet in large measure the controversy is due to a lack of
appropriate theory to account for disequilibrium dynamics that can persist for years or even
decades. Of course, theory and data are entwined in a feedback loop without theory to guide
empirical tests, little evidence for disequilibrium dynamics such as long cycles was collected, without compelling evidence of long cycles, there was little motivation to develop new theory Recent
years have witnessed a dramatic change in both the theories available to model nonlinear, disequilibrium dynamics such as long waves and the data supporting their existence The existence and

---

[1] Ultimately, of course, growth of population and material production will cease as the world makes a transition to
a post-industrial economy consistent with various social, environmental and ecological limits Debate continues as
to the proximity of the limits to growth, the likely dynamics of the transition from growth, and the sustainability of
different economic and social systems (Meadows, Meadows, and Randers 1992)

causes of the long wave are now reasonably well established, and theory is emerging to understand how the different cyclical modes in the economy interact with one another

One of the principal mysteries theorists have faced is why there seem to be only a few distinct periodicities rather than cycles at all frequencies And how might the different cyclical modes interact? Could, as Schumpeter (1939) argued, the coincident downturn of the business cycle, construction cycle, and long wave account for the severity of the Great Depression? More fundamentally, why should the frequencies of these cycles have (roughly) commensurate periods, so that their downturns might coincide? Indeed, even if one admits the possibility that individual firms might generate cyclical movements, the different parameters characterizing the structure and decision making processes of different firms would cause them to oscillate with different frequencies and phases Why then should there be aggregate cyclical movements at all?

Unfortunately, macroeconomic theory has been largely silent on the issues of multiple modes, synchronization, and entrainment The problem resides both in the prevailing assumptions of rationality and equilibrium, neither of which are good approximations to actual economic systems, and in the tools used to analyze economic dynamics Over the past few decades an impressive body of evidence has accumulated documenting the bounds on human rationality (Simon 1982) Experimental and field studies in psychology, economics and other social sciences have documented a wide range of heuristics people use to make decisions in complex environments, and the many systematic errors and biases that result (Kahneman, Slovic, and Tversky 1982, Hogarth 1987) Appropriate theories of economic dynamics, and economic behavior in general, should embody models of decision making consistent with empirical knowledge (including qualitative data and field study as well as econometric analysis) of the processes of judgment and choice managers actually use (Simon 1979, Sterman 1987, Morecroft 1985).

The analytical tools traditionally used to study economic dynamics have also slowed understanding Though many macroeconomic models of the business cycle exist, few address the issue of multiple cyclical modes In part, this is because difference equations have dominated dynamic analysis (see Samuelson 1947, p 380), and many difference equation models do not explicitly identify the unit of time between 'periods' (e g Samuelson 1939, Goodwin 1951) so that the structures, parameters, and behavior of such models cannot be validated It is simply presumed that the cycles of these models are the short-term business cycle (see Low 1980 for a critique)

More important, despite notable early exceptions (e g Goodwin 1951, Kaldor 1940), until recently most models of economic cycles were linear or nearly linear (see e g Day 1982, Lorenz 1989, Semmler 1989 for modern nonlinear approaches) But linear theory is not an appropriate foundation for the study of economic dynamics (Forrester 1987) First, economic systems distinguish themselves from most systems considered in the natural sciences by the prevalence of positive feedback loops Well known examples include the accelerator and multiplier loops of Keynesian theory Other positive loops operate through extrapolative expectations, agglomeration effects, increasing returns, the effect of inflation expectations on real interest rates and thus aggregate demand, speculation and financial crises, and synergies and standards formation among and within technologies for production, communication, and organization (Sterman 1986a, Graham and Senge 1980, Arthur 1988, Semmler 1989) Such positive feedbacks create the possibility of strongly nonlinear behavior the positive loops may destabilize otherwise convergent processes of adjustment which then grow in amplitude until constrained by various nonlinearities Such phenomena cannot be understood by means of linear or nearly-linear models

Furthermore, if the economic system were linear, the cycles produced by different firms, industries, and nations would evolve independently of one another and the total behavior would be the linear superposition of the independent modes While individual firms might exhibit fluctuations, the aggregate of many independently oscillating firms might be quite constant – there would be no business cycle as a macroeconomic phenomenon While diffusion of business cycles has received considerable empirical attention, theoretical understanding of synchronization has lagged Thus many theories find the cause of synchronization in common sources of external variation, either government monetary and fiscal policies, changes in aggregate demand, or highly correlated shocks and expectations (Burns 1969, Mitchell 1927, Zarnowitz 1985 provides a survey)

Modern dynamical theory offers another explanation nonlinear mode locking In nonlinear systems, superposition does not hold Instead, the periodicities of coupled oscillators may adjust to one another to achieve a rational ratio, or winding number Mode locking has recently attracted considerable interest in the natural sciences, especially since it has been established that mode locking possesses a number of universal features independent of the particular system under study (Jensen, Bak, and Bohr 1983, 1984). The same processes of entrainment have been observed, for instance, in paced nerve cells (Colding-Jorgensen 1983), externally stimulated heart cells (Glass, Shrier, and Belair 1986), fluid dynamics (Glazier et al 1986), coupled thermostatically controlled radiators (Togeby, et al. 1988), and forced microwave diodes (Mosekilde et al 1990) Mode locking provides an explanation for the entrainment of economic fluctuations that is more robust than prior explanations, and creates the possibility of nonlinear phenomena such as period-doubling bifurcations, simultaneous multiple periodic solutions, and deterministic chaos Mode locking also gives rise to the 'devil's staircase', an unusual fractal structure we describe below

We begin by reviewing the stylized facts of the different cycles, then discuss the behavioral foundations for each mode at the micro level We focus on the longer cycles as these are the most controversial and least understood, particularly the economic long wave We survey the principal theories of the economic long wave that have emerged in the past decade, specifically the integrated theory developed by the MIT System Dynamics Group and the neo-Schumpeterian innovation theories. To illustrate the type of behavioral, nonlinear disequilibrium theory we advocate, we present a simple model of the long wave and show how the wave arises through interactions among locally rational decision rules embedded in a nonlinear feedback system.

Next, we use the model to consider interactions among the modes. The theory of nonlinear entrainment and mode locking sheds light on why there are a small number of modes rather than cycles of all frequencies, and why there are aggregate movements at all rather than firm or industry level cycles that wash out at the macroeconomic level We conclude with implications for the development of empirically grounded, behavioral, disequilibrium theories of economic dynamics

2. Economic Dynamics: Multiple Modes of Behavior

The most thoroughly analyzed cyclical mode in the economy is the short-term (3-7 year) business cycle (Mitchell 1927, Gordon 1951, Moore 1961, Zarnowitz 1985), illustrated in figure 1 by US industrial production and civilian unemployment for the period 1947 to 1992 With characteristic phase shifts and amplitudes, the short-term business cycle manifests clearly in a host of aggregates and industry level data including capacity utilization, inventory coverage, help wanted advertising, interest rates, etc Among the well-known characteristics of the short-term cycle is the phenomenon of amplification, in which the amplitude of the cycle increases as one moves from the production of consumer goods to intermediates to raw materials (figure 2) Theories of the short-term cycle should explain these details as well as generate a fluctuation in output with the appropriate period, amplitude, phase relations, and variability

Many time series also provide evidence for the existence of a 15-25 year construction (or Kuznets) cycle (Riggleman 1933, Hoyt 1933, Long 1940, Kuznets 1973) An example is given in figure 3 showing the vacancy rate of commercial office space in Boston from 1952 to 1990 Similar cycles can also be found, for instance, in production capacity of the paper industry (Randers 1984) or in capacity utilization of the world oil tanker fleet (Bakken 1992) At the industry or regional level, the amplitude of the construction cycle is often so high that nonlinearities are clearly involved.For example, during bust periods the rate of new construction falls nearly to zero for extended periods, and excess capacity declines at a rate constrained by the lifetime of capital stocks

Let us consider the processes that produce these two distinct modes We focus, initially, on the dynamics of individual firms, and later consider how such firms may become entrained with one another and with the government, consumer, and financial sectors to produce a coherent aggregate cycle Consider a manufacturing firm in equilibrium, assuming for simplicity that the firm is small relative to the labor, capital and other input markets, so that factor prices can be considered constant Now consider the firm's response to an unanticipated step increase in incoming orders The company will eventually expand output to meet orders. In the long run, production, material consumption, work force and capital stock all rise in proportion to incoming orders The question is how the transient will unfold.

If all inputs could be adjusted immediately, the transient would be fast and nonoscillatory However, factor inputs cannot change instantly Backlogs and inventories buffer the production line from short term variations in demand to provide time for efficient adjustment of inputs In fact, immediately following the demand shock the firm may not change production at all, until it becomes clear that incoming orders will remain at the new, higher level Inventories necessarily fall Optimal inventory may also increase as the expected throughput rises To restore inventory to desired levels, the firm must increase production above the rate of incoming orders for at least some period of time As a consequence, orders for materials and intermediate goods must also increase above the rate of incoming orders, passing a larger disturbance on to the supplying industries This process, the familiar inventory accelerator, provides an explanation for the amplification of the business cycle from the consumer goods sector through the intermediate goods and finally to the raw materials sector (T. Mitchell 1923, Metzler 1941, Forrester 1961, Mass 1975)

The amplification of demand shocks at each stage of production is an inevitable consequence of three fundamental features of production: (1) the existence of decision-making and physical delays in adjusting production to demand shocks (e g forecasting and administrative lags, lags in factor acquisition), (2) the existence of stocks such as inventories, work in process, and backlogs which buffer the difference between orders and output, and (3) the need to adjust these stocks towards target values when shocks occur (to restore inventory to initial levels after an unanticipated demand increase, output must rise above shipments for a time)

The inevitability of amplification, however, does not mean that oscillation is similarly inevitable (by oscillation is meant a system that is less than critically damped) The existence, stability, and frequency of oscillatory response to demand shocks depends on the nature of the feedback processes by which a firm adjusts output to demand, as well as the myriad couplings among the firm, its suppliers, customers, and other actors in the economy

Provided that needed materials are available, small changes in output may be accomplished quickly through more intensive use of existing employees (overtime) From a control-theoretic point of view, the use of workweek to regulate inventory creates an effectively first-order negative feedback loop which is non-oscillatory and adds damping to the system (Sterman 1988) However, the workweek response is nonlinear it is limited by the cost of overtime, by decreasing worker productivity after long work weeks, and ultimately by the length of the day Thus, while small amplitude changes in demand can be accommodated through overtime, larger and more persistent changes saturate the workweek feedback, requiring expansion of the work force

Expanding the work force, however, involves significant delays Vacancies must be authorized, new employees hired and trained, and time must pass before productivity rises to that of experienced workers (comparable delays exist in the case of an unexpected decrease in demand) The use of employment to control inventory levels and respond to demand shocks creates a negative feedback loop, but unlike the work week loop, the employment adjustment loop involves delays on the order of several months or more Negative feedback loops with such phase lag elements are oscillatory The characteristic behavior of models that portray workweek and work force adjustments with realistic decision parameters is damped oscillations with a period of 3 to 7 years (Forrester 1961, Mass 1975) These models also generate the phase (lead and lag) and amplitude relationships observed in the data for output, employment, inventories, delivery delay, vacancies, labor accession and separation flows, and other variables The business cycle these models generate is robust as the boundary of the model expands to include consumer demand, interest rates, monetary and fiscal policies, and other elements of the traditional aggregate supply/aggregate demand model (Mass 1975, N. Forrester 1982)

Regulation of output by workforce adjustment is also limited due to diminishing returns as labor expands relative to existing plant and equipment. In the long run, capital stocks must also be increased. However, capital investment involves even longer delays arising from the process of planning for, ordering and constructing new plant and equipment. Adjustment of capital stocks thus involves a negative feedback loop with substantially longer delays. Models that integrate capital investment with inventory and work force management tend to produce oscillations with periods of 15-25 years in addition to the short-term cycle (Mass 1975, N Forrester 1982, Low 1980)

The theory described so far assumes agents have bounded rationality in the sense of Simon (1979, 1982) Agents seek to take appropriate decisions, but do not possess the cognitive and other resources necessary to approach optimality, even in the weak rational expectations sense, due to the complexity of the high order, nonlinear, randomly-excited dynamic system in which they operate The theory of bounded rationality, as applied here, recognizes that firms partition the total problem of optimizing the enterprise into subproblems. Production is typically influenced by decisions at the plant level, while pricing may be the responsibility of senior divisional management and capital investment may be decided at corporate headquarters. Due to limitations of time, information availability, and attentional resources, management of the subsystems may be imperfectly coordinated. The theory of bounded rationality does not assume that the individual managers are irrational but rather locally or intendedly rational – that is, they use heuristics that would work well if the couplings among subsystems were weak and the separability assumption implicit in task factoring and decision making within the firm were valid (Sterman 1985, 1987, Morecroft 1985)

Extensive experimental evidence shows that the bounds on rational decision making in dynamic systems are severe. In simple experimental economies such as the classical multiplier-accelerator model (Sterman 1989a), inventory management (Diehl 1992), or distribution of a commodity

(Sterman 1989b), subjects perform well below optimal and generate systematic, persistent and costly oscillations These systematic decision errors become more severe as the feedback complexity of the environment increases, particularly as delays lengthen (Diehl 1992, Paich and Sterman 1992, Brehmer 1990) Experience, incentives, and market institutions moderate but do not eliminate these errors (Paich and Sterman 1992, Kampmann and Sterman 1992, Smith, Suchanek and Williams 1988)

3   The economic long wave

The third main cyclical mode of economic behavior is the economic long wave or Kondratieff cycle The long wave is the most controversial and least understood of the three cyclical modes It is also the most important. The long wave is far larger in amplitude than the business cycle, and of such great duration that the stresses it generates cannot be contained within the market system, but rather influence the evolution of, and sometimes the revolutions in, the institutional structure of the world economic and political system (Sterman 1992, 1986a) The Russian economist N D Kondratieff (1928/1984, 1935) was one of the first to draw attention to the wave-like character of industrial development, with alternating periods of relative affluence and economic hardship Using data on commodity prices, interest rates, industrial production, raw materials consumption, and foreign trade, Kondratieff argued for the existence of a roughly 60 year cyclic motion, and speculated that it was related to investment in long-lived capital

The economic stagnation and crises of the last two decades and the inability of conventional economic policies to restore former balances have prompted renewed interest in the long wave and many new theories of its origin (Freeman 1982, van Duijn 1983, Vasko 1987) However, the long wave remains controversial among economists Most have taken a rather agnostic stance concerning the existence of long waves, maintaining that historical evidence for long fluctuations of sufficient regularity to be considered cyclic is unconvincing (Garvy 1943, Mansfield 1983, Rosenberg and Frischtak 1983) While few deny that the performance of industrialized economies expenences significant long term vanations, many economists see these more as the outcome of particular historical events such as wars or gold discovenes than as a result of endogenous processes In contrast, recent studies by Bieshaar and Kleinknecht (1984) and by Rasmussen et al (1989) designed to test the Kondratieff hypothesis in real series arrive at generally positive results, and Sterman (1986a) reports a wide range of data consistent with the long wave hypothesis Today, most students of long cycles agree that the historic depression periods were the 1830s and 1840s, the 1870s through late 1890s, the 1920s and 1930s, and the period from about 1974 through (at least) the early 1990s (van Duijn 1983, Vasko 1987, Goldstein 1988)

To illustrate, Figure 4 shows detrended real GNP in the United States from 1947 to 1992 After removal of the long-term exponential growth trend what remains are the cyclical modes, particularly the short-term business cycle and the long wave The post-war long wave is clearly visible, with GNP growing faster than trend from the end of World War II through about 1970, and slower than trend since The business cycle, with much smaller amplitude than the long wave, appears as small ripples on the great swell of the long wave. Note also how the phase of the long wave conditions the apparent seventy of the business cycle During the expansion of the long wave, periods of business cycle expansion seem to be long and vigorous, while recessions are thought to be short and mild, as the rising tide of the long wave lifts all boats During the downturn phase of the long wave, recessions seem to be longer and deeper, and the growth phase of the business cycle appears to be weaker An analyst unaware of the long wave would conclude that the character of the business cycle had changed as the long wave peaked and began to decline

Kondratieff viewed the long wave as a manifestation of essential forces in the capitalist economy, and argued that a broad spectrum of social and economic phenomena were shaped by the wave In particular, each burst of capital expansion would allow a new set of technologies to be exploited While accepting the general idea of endogenously generated long waves, Schumpeter (1939) articulated the opposite causality between economic growth and technological innovation For Schumpeter, innovations create the products and markets that drive economic growth

Both lines of thought continue today One of the earliest and most thoroughly tested formal models of the long wave has been developed at MIT's System Dynamics Group (Forrester 1976, 1977, 1979, 1981, Graham and Senge 1980, Sterman 1985, 1986a, 1986b, 1987, 1988, 1989a, 1990, 1992) The theory integrates a variety of economic processes, both real and nominal, including capital investment, employment, work force participation, wages, inflation, interest rates, monetary policy, debt, and consumer demand, among others The MIT model endogenously generates the long wave as well as the short-term business cycle, construction cycle, and other modes including economic growth and the expansion of the government sector relative to the private economy A simple version of this model is analyzed below

In parallel with this line of economic modeling, neo-Schumpeterian theories stressing the role of technological innovation as causes of the long wave have been developed Mensch (1979) argues fundamental scientific discoveries and new inventions occur more or less randomly But for an invention to acquire economic significance, innovation, or the commercialization of the invention, must occur The rate of basic innovations, those which plant the seeds of new industries, is conditioned by the state of the economy During long wave upturns, economic growth is rapid and the existing infrastructure is highly productive· incentives to invest in new technologies are small At the same time, positive network externalities and commitment to existing infrastructure make it difficult to introduce alternative transport, communication or energy systems Long wave downturns arise when the potential of existing technologies saturates Switching costs then decline, producing a burst of basic innovation as many of the inventions accumulated during the upswing now find practical application The resulting swarm of innovations launches new industries and provides the impetus for the next upswing Formal mathematical models of these neo-Schumpeterian theories include Montaño and Ebeling (1980), Mosekilde and Rasmussen (1986), Silverberg (1988) and Dosi (1988), Kleinknecht (1984) provides some empirical tests One difficulty in innovation theories of the long wave is explaining why disparate technologies in disparate contexts and markets should reach saturation in synchrony after 40-60 years, cycle after cycle Addressing this problem, Graham and Senge (1980) integrated innovation theories with the MIT model and argue innovation rates are entrained by the endogenous economic processes that generate the long wave Other authors have related the long wave to changes in employment and wages (Freeman et al. 1982), resource scarcity (Rostow 1978), class struggle (Mandel 1980), and war (Goldstein 1988)

4. A simple behavioral model of the long wave

A control-theoretic explanation for the long wave emerging from the MIT theory can be divided into two parts· first, as described above, acquisition of capacity in individual firms involves inherently oscillatory processes In isolation, these processes are stable, producing damped oscillations when excited by exogenous changes in demand However, a wide range of self-reinforcing processes exist in the linkages between firms and among the production, financial, household and government sectors of the economy, destabilizing the cycle and lengthening its period Demand for capital increases the capacity needs of the capital producing industries, further boosting orders for capital For example, expansion by capital producers raises labor demand and wages, leading to substitution of capital for labor and still greater demand for capital. Rising aggregate demand boosts prices, reducing real interest rates and further stimulating investment Rising output boosts income and aggregate demand, further boosting output Expansion leads to expectations of future growth, leading to further investment and output growth Rising credit demand to finance the boom causes monetary accommodation, additional inflation, and still lower real interest rates And so on These positive loops include many familiar processes including the Keynesian income multiplier, the Mundell effect, and Fisher's (1933) debt/deflation spiral The full MIT national model integrates these and other feedback processes (Sterman 1986a and 1988 provide details)

Model analyses (Rasmussen, Mosekilde and Sterman 1985, Brøns and Sturis 1991) show that these positive feedbacks cause a Hopf-bifurcation through which the equilibrium of the economy becomes unstable Any perturbations cause divergent oscillations that are eventually bounded by nonlinearities such as the nonnegativity of gross investment and limits on capacity utilization of the capital stock, producing a limit cycle The long wave appears to be a self-sustaining oscillation that, although influenced by shocks and perturbations, does not require external excitation to persist In contrast, the short-term business cycle appears to be a stable, damped mode that requires external excitation, as in Frisch (1933)

One of the most fundamental self-reinforcing feedbacks is the capital investment multiplier, or 'capital self-ordering', the fact that in the aggregate the capital producing sector of the economy orders and acquires plant and equipment from itself If the demand for consumer goods and services increases, the consumer goods industry must expand its capacity and so places orders for new factories, machinery, vehicles, etc To supply the high volume of orders, the capital producing sector must also expand its capital stock and hence places orders for more buildings, machines, rolling stock, trucks, etc , causing the total demand for capital to rise still further in a self-reinforcing spiral of increasing orders, a greater need for expansion, and still more orders

In equilibrium, the multiplier effect of capital self-ordering is modest (Sterman 1985) However, the long wave is an inherently disequilibrium phenomenon, and during transient adjustments the strength of self-ordering becomes much greater than in equilibrium This is partly a consequence of the classical investment accelerator During disequilibrium a variety of additional positive feed-back loops further augment the demand for capital These include

(i) Amplification caused by inventory and backlog adjustments· Rising orders deplete the inven-tories and swell the backlogs of capital-sector firms, leading to further pressure to expand and still more orders During the downturn, low backlogs and involuntary inventory accumulation further depress demand, leading to still more excess inventory

(ii) Amplification caused by rising lead time for capital During the long wave expansion, the demand for capital outstrips capacity Capital producers find it takes longer than anticipated to acquire new capacity, causing capacity to lag further behind desired levels, creating still more pres-sure to order, and further swelling the demand for capital

(iii) Amplification caused by growth expectations: Growing demand, rising backlogs, and long lead times during the long wave expansion all encourage expectations of additional growth in demand for capital Expectations of growth lead to additional investments, further swelling demand in a self-fulfilling prophecy During the downturn, pessimism further undercuts investment

Sterman (1985) developed a behavioral model capturing the destabilizing positive feedback caused by capital self-ordering The model is designed to isolate the minimum structure sufficient to generate the long wave with realistic parameter values It does not include the full range of feedbacks included in the MIT model However simulations with more comprehensive versions have shown that the characteristic behavior produced by the simple model is robust to structural elaboration of the model It is also possible to find more complicated modes of behavior as the model is extended (Mosekilde et al 1992) and disaggregated (Kampmann 1984)

The model creates a two-sector economy with a capital producing and goods producing sector The focus is the capital investment accelerator Goodwin (1951, 4) notes that the traditional acceleration principle assumes

> that actual, realized capital stock is maintained at the desired relation with output. We know in reality that it is seldom so, there being now too much and now too little capital stock For this there are two good reasons The rate of investment is limited by the capacity of the investment goods industry At the other extreme there is an even more inescapable and effective limit. Machines, once made, cannot be unmade, so that negative investment is limited to attrition from wear Therefore capital stock cannot be increased fast enough in the upswing, nor decreased fast enough in the downswing, so that at one time we have shortages and rationing of orders and at the other excess capacity with idle plants and machines

A single factor of production (capital plant and equipment) is considered. The model includes, however, an explicit representation of the capital acquisition delay (construction lag) and the capacity of the investment goods sector As a result, orders for and acquisition of capital are not necessarily equal, and at any moment there will typically be a supply line of capital under construction For simplicity, the demand for capital of the goods-producing sector is exogenous, and there is no representation of the consumption multiplier

We first describe the equations for the capital producer, then the couplings between sectors The model allows for variable utilization of the capital stock. Thus production P depends on utilization of production capacity C Utilization is a nonlinear function of the ratio of desired production P* to capacity Desired output P* is determined by the total backlog of unfilled orders B and the normal delivery delay Δ* Capacity is proportional to the capital stock K, with capital/output ratio κ

$$P = u(P^*/C)C \, , \, u(0) = 0, \, u(1) = 1, \, u' \geq 0, \, u'' \leq 0, \, u(\infty) = u^{max} \tag{1}$$

$$P^* = B/\Delta^* \tag{2}$$

$$C = K/\kappa \tag{3}$$

The capital stock of the capital sector is augmented by acquisitions A and diminished by discards D Discards are exponential with average lifetime τ

$$(d/dt)K = A - D \tag{4}$$

$$D = K/\tau \tag{5}$$

The acquisition of capital depends on the firm's supply line of unfilled orders for capital S and the capital acquisition lag Λ

$$A = S/\Lambda \tag{6}$$

The supply line of capital under construction represents the orders for capital plant and equipment, O_k, the firm has placed but not yet received

$$(d/dt)S = O_k - A \tag{7}$$

Thus far the model describes the stock and flow structure of the firm and the physical limits on capacity utilization The key behavioral formulation is the decision rule for capital orders O_k

$$O_k = K \, f(O_k^*/K), \qquad 0 \leq f(\cdot) \leq f^{max}, \, f' \geq 0 \tag{8}$$

$$O_k{}^* = D + \alpha_k(K^* - K) + \alpha_s(S^* - S) \tag{9}$$

here the actual order rate depends nonlinearly on the indicated order rate $O_k{}^*$ as a fraction per year of existing capital stock K, ensuring that orders remain nonnegative even if there is a large surplus of capital. Due to limits on e g financing, absorption capacity, etc , orders are limited to a maximum fraction of existing capacity f^{max}, as in Goodwin (1951). Three motivations for investment are assumed· (1) to replace discards, (2) to correct any discrepancy between the desired capital stock K^* and the actual stock K, and (3) to correct any discrepancy between the desired supply line of capital under construction S^* and the actual supply line S The adjustment parameters α_k and α_s determine the aggressiveness of the response to discrepancies To ensure an appropriate acquisition rate of new capital, firms must maintain a supply line proportional to the delay they face in acquiring capital Thus the desired supply line is proportional to the capital acquisition lag Λ and the current capital discard rate D (see Sterman 1989a and 1989b for details and experimental evidence supporting this formulation)

$$S^* = \Lambda D \tag{10}$$

The desired capital stock K^* is a nonlinear function of desired output P^*

$$K^* = K_0 \, g\{\kappa P^*/K_0\}, \qquad g\{0\} = 0, \, g\{1\} = 1, \, g' \geq 0, \, g'' \leq 0 \tag{11}$$

Desired capital stock is assumed to rise proportionately with desired output for small deviations from the equilibrium value K_0, but diminishing returns to capital are assumed to limit capital expansion when $\kappa P^*/K_0$ becomes large.

Finally, the backlog of the firm is augmented by customer orders O and reduced by output P

$$(d/dt)B = O - P \tag{12}$$

and the actual delivery delay of the firm, Δ, is determined by the average residence time of orders ın the backlog,

$$\Delta = B/P \tag{13}$$

Equations (1) - (13) descrıbe a sımple model of a firm The model ıncludes an explıcıt delay ın acquırıng capıtal stock and realıstıc nonlınearıtıes represen   using basıc physıcal processes such as nonnegatıvıty of gross ınvestment and lımıts to utılızatıon of exıstıng capacıty Sterman (1985) shows the ındıvıdual decısıon rules of the model are ıntendedly ratıonal, and ınvestıgates ıts sensı- tıvıty to parameters Wıth realıstıc parameters for a capıtal producıng firm ($\kappa=3$, $\Lambda = \Delta = 1\ 5$, $\tau =$ 20, $\alpha_k = 3$, and $\alpha_s = 3$) and exogenous orders O, the transıent response of the model to shocks ıs a hıghly damped oscıllatıon wıth a perıod of about 20 years As descrıbed above, the cycle arıses from the negatıve feedback loop by whıch output ıs regulated through changes ın productıon capacıty, wıth a lag caused by the capıtal acquısıtıon delay The model does not produce the short- term busıness cycle because labor ıs not explıcıtly treated, productıon P ınstantly adjusts to the desıred rate P^* as long as the firm ıs not capacıty constraıned

To see how the long wave mıght arıse through capıtal self-orderıng, we now modıfy the model to represent the entıre capıtal-producıng sector of an economy In the aggregate the capıtal sector orders capıtal from ıtself, so the total rate at whıch new orders for capıtal are receıved O ıs now the sum of the capıtal sector's orders for capıtal, O_k, and orders for capıtal placed by the goods sector, O_g, whıch represents all other purchasers of capıtal plant and equıpment

$$O = O_k + O_g \tag{14}$$

The backlog of unfilled orders for capıtal ıs now the sum of the supply lınes of the capıtal and goods sectors

$$B = S + S_g \tag{12'}$$

where S_g ıs the supply lıne of unfilled orders for capıtal placed by the firms ın the goods sector

$$(d/dt)S_g = (O_g - A_g) \tag{15}$$

The rate at which the goods sector acquires capital depends on the goods sector's supply line S_g and the delivery delay of the capital sector Δ

$$A_g = S_g/\Delta \tag{16}$$

Likewise, since the capital sector acquires capital from itself, the capital acquisition lag, Λ, it faces is its own delivery delay, Δ

$$\Lambda = \Delta \tag{17}$$

Finally, the demand for capital derived from the goods sector of the economy O_g is exogenous

The full model is a third order nonlinear differential equation system (the state variables are K, S, and S_g) It captures some of the positive feedbacks created by the dependence of the capital sector of any economy on its own output. As shown in Sterman (1985) and Brøns and Sturis (1991), due to these positive feedbacks the equilibrium of the model is unstable With the same parameters as above and constant orders from the goods sector, O_g, a small perturbation produces expanding oscillations which are ultimately bounded by the nonlinear constraints associated with the investment function g{ } and capacity utilization function u{ } The steady state behavior of the model is a limit cycle with a period of approximately 50 years (Figure 5) The long wave generated by the model has many of the features of the long wave generated by the full MIT model, including phase relationships and relative amplitudes for output, capital stocks, capital orders, acquisitions and discards, delivery delay, and capacity utilization A full equation listing, explanation of formulations, and sensitivity tests are found in Sterman (1985)

The *cycle* arises via the lagged negative feedback loop described in the discussion of the construction cycle. To understand how the oscillation *sustains* itself, consider the processes that produce the upper and lower turning points in the cycle. Imagine that the equilibrium is disturbed by a small increase in the demand derived from the goods sector The capital producing sector finds it

has insufficient capacity and therefore increases its own orders above the replacement rate The

total demand for capital thus increases still further above capacity, stimulating orders still more

Total orders rise faster than capacity due to the construction delay, so the backlog of unfilled orders

rises, and capital producers find their attempts to expand are slowed by rising delivery delays The

gap between desired and actual capital widens further, causing still more orders to be placed

These feedbacks generate a self-reinforcing spiral of increasing orders, a greater need for capital

and still more orders Eventually, the various nonlinearities limit the increase in demand

Production capacity gradually overtakes orders The backlog then starts to fall Now the same

positive loops that powered the expansion drive the economy into depression With decreasing

backlogs, desired production capacity starts to fall, leading to a reduction in orders Falling deliv-

ery delays reduce orders by accelerating acquisitions and reducing the required supply line Thus

the capital sector finds itself with excess capacity and cuts its orders for capital, further decreasing

the demand for capital and leading to still more cutbacks in orders At the end of the upswing, the

capital producing sector has severe excess capacity and cuts its own orders to zero Capital pro-

duction must remain below the level required for replacements until the excess capacity depreciates

– a process which may take a decade or more due to the long lifetime of the capital stock

The lower turning point and initiation of the next cycle are direct consequences of bounded

rationality The model assumes capital producers build capacity to meet the order rate they forecast

and do not understand or invest to satisfy the general equilibrium of the full economy

Specifically, during the depression phase of the long cycle demand for capital is less than the sys-

tem's equilibrium because the capital sector itself is ordering less than discards Eventually capac-

ity approaches the level required to meet the demand of the goods sector Capital producers then

increase their orders in order to offset discards However, the increase in orders boosts the total

demand for capital above capacity, and backlogs begin to rise Faced now with capacity too low to

fill incoming orders from the goods sector and its own orders, the capital sector must increase its own orders further above replacement needs, and the next expansion begins

Thus the long wave is generated endogenously by the investment behavior of the capital producing sector, and persists without exogenous excitation Changing the parameters of the model such as, for instance, the capital/output ratio or the maxima of the nonlinear functions may change the amplitude and period of the wave However, the characteristic self-sustained oscillation with a period on the order of 50 years is robust over most of the realistic parameter range Beyond this range various bifurcations (i e changes in the steady-state behavior of the model) occur (Rasmussen et al 1985, Szymkat and Mosekilde 1989, Brøns and Sturis 1991)

The model, particularly the critical decision rule for capital investment, has been tested both econometrically and experimentally. Senge (1980) showed that a disequilibrium investment function similar to the rule here provides a better account of post-war US data for a variety of industries than the neoclassical investment function Sterman (1987, 1989a) converted the model into an experiment in which subjects, including some experienced managers, made the capital investment decision for the capital producing sector Despite full information, the vast majority of the subjects generated long wave cycles corresponding closely to those of the model Econometric estimation of the subjects' decisions showed they conformed well to the assumed decision rule for capital orders Simulation showed that the estimated decision rules for about 40% of the subjects produced the limit cycle behavior, and about 25% yielded deterministic chaos (Sterman 1989c) Subsequent experiments have shown these effects to be robust to financial incentives, training, experience, and the presence of market institutions (Diehl 1992, Kampmann and Sterman 1992)

5. Interacting cycles: Nonlinear entrainment and mode locking

The discussion above provides a disequilibrium, behavioral foundation for each of the three main cyclical modes in the economy. Thus far, each mode has been discussed separately If the economy were linear, the cycles generated by each firm would evolve independently of one another, and the total behavior would be a simple superposition Each firm might generate fluctuations with a characteristic power spectrum in response to various disturbances in the environment But to the extent such variations were imperfectly correlated across firms, the cyclical movements of independent firms would tend to average out at the industry and macroeconomic levels In such a world the only way a coherent aggregate business cycle could come about is through common sources of exogenous variation, such as government monetary and fiscal policies or highly correlated shocks or expectations, and indeed there are many such theories of business cycles (Burns 1969, Mitchell 1927, Zarnowitz 1985 provides a survey)

However, there are strong theoretical arguments to suggest that nonlinearity plays a crucial role in bringing about interaction between the modes and thereby shaping the overall behavior Even at the level of the individual firm, the nonlinear limits on the workweek and work force adjustment processes tend to couple the short and long term modes to one another Other nonlinearities arise from nonnegativity constraints on gross investment, shipments of goods from inventory, etc , from upper limits to capacity utilization, hiring and investment rates, and because these decisions depend nonlinearly on multiple cues

The empirical evidence for nonlinear interactions between the various modes is also strong As an example figure 6a shows the variation in oil-tanker spot rates from 1950 through 1991 Spot rates are characterized by series of sharp peaks and deep valleys occurring at 3 to 5 year intervals, separated by periods of 10-15 years in which rates and their variance are low During the peaks, which often last for only a few months, rates of more than 400 are attained while during the depression periods rates are as low as 40. The alternating pattern of calm punctuated by wild swings reflects the nonlinear interaction of the tanker construction cycle with business cycle variations in the demand for oil transportation The construction cycle in this case arises from the long delays in the ordering and building of new tankers

Econometric, experimental and field studies show that ship-owner's decisions to order new tankers are primarily based on the recent tanker rate (Zannetos 1966, Randers 1984, Bakken 1992)

Suppose demand for oil shipment is high relative to the capacity of the world fleet. Tanker rates will be high The resulting high profits induce existing operators to expand their fleets and cause entry of new players into the market. Orders for new ships swell. However, due to the long construction delay (2-4 years), demand will remain high for several years, during which time additional new orders are placed by existing players and new entrants When these ships are commissioned excess capacity develops and tanker rates fall New orders drop below scrap rates (often nearly reaching zero), but since the service life of typical tankers is 15-25 years, spot rates and new construction remain depressed for years, until capacity once again drops below demand, rates rise, and the next cycle begins Consistent with the theory of bounded rationality, this description assumes shipowners do not have complete information about the global shipbuilding market or understanding of long-term market dynamics, but rely primarily on current profit potential (spot rates relative to costs of new ships) in placing orders (Zannetos 1966, Bakken 1992)

The nonlinear interaction of the business and construction cycles is shown by comparing figure 6a to figure 6b Spot rates are low and insensitive to the business cycle in periods of surplus tanker capacity, since demand fluctuations are easily accommodated by higher utilization (the short run elasticity of supply is high) Conversely, rates are high and volatile when capacity utilization for the world fleet is high High utilization means supply is quite inelastic in the short run, small variations in demand caused by the business cycle or by geopolitical shocks yield dramatic changes in spot rates The parameters governing the response of the market to short term variations in demand including the business cycle depend on the phase of the long construction cycle Thus the Suez crisis, coming at a time of high fleet utilization, caused surges in rates, while the Iran-Iraq war, coming during a time of excess capacity, is barely visible in the data

Nonlinear dynamical theory also suggests that the different cyclic modes may entrain one another through the process of mode-locking Specifically, oscillatory modes in nonlinear systems with similar frequencies tend to adjust to one another such that their periods become precisely the same The classical example is the synchronization of the rotational motion of the moon to its orbital motion, so that the same hemisphere of the moon perpetually faces the earth Other well-known examples are the synchronization of the circadian rhythm of many organisms to the 24 hour cycle of night and day, the synchronization of (mechanical) clocks hanging on the same wall, and the synchronization of menstrual cycles between women living in close contact Nonlinear coupling of different oscillators can thus explain why there are aggregate business cycles when the differing parameters and initial states of different firms might cause them to oscillate with different frequencies and phases, averaging out at the macroeconomic level Couplings between firms cause the cycles generated by different firms to be drawn together into a coherent aggregate cycle with stable phase relations (Forrester 1977) Homer (1980) shows how basic market processes such as consumer response to relative price and availability provide sufficient coupling to synchronize firms with different parameters and initial phases

Synchronization is only one manifestation of the more general phenomenon of frequency-locking or nonlinear entrainment (Arnol'd 1965, Glass et al 1984, Jensen et al 1983, 1984, Rand et al 1982, Mosekilde et al 1990) In nonlinear systems, an oscillatory mode contains various harmonics, and two modes may synchronize whenever a harmonic of one mode is close to a harmonic of the other As a result, nonlinear oscillators tend to lock to one another such that one oscillator completes precisely p cycles each time the other oscillator completes q cycles, where p and q are integers Such mode locking might explain Schumpeter's (1939) observation that the period of the construction cycle was approximately three times the period of the business cycles, and the period of the long wave was approximately three times the period of the construction cycle

To illustrate nonlinear entrainment and explore how the different cyclical modes might interact, we modify the long wave model so that orders for capital derived from the goods sector fluctuate sinusoidally with period T and fractional amplitude A around a constant level O_g^*

$$O_g = O_g^*(1 + A\sin(2\pi t/T)) \tag{18}$$

The sinusoidal forcing models in a simple fashion the other cyclical modes generated by the economy Faced with this forcing, the frequency of the long wave will adjust in a manner that depends both on the amplitude and frequency of the external forcing The adjustment will tend to lock the two cycles into an overall periodic motion in which the long wave completes precisely p cycles each time the forcing signal completes q cycles, where p and q are integers

As an example figure 7a shows the results obtained when the model is perturbed by a 20 per cent (A = 0 20) sinusoidal modulation with a forcing period T = 22 2 years Here the forcing frequency is representative of the construction cycle Relative to the unforced limit cycle behavior (figure 5), the long wave has increased its period by close to 40% so as to accommodate precisely 3 periods of the faster cycle Moreover, within the interval 19 9 years < T < 24 8 years, a change in the period of the forcing signal will cause a precisely proportional shift in the long wave such that the 1.3 entrainment is maintained

F1b 7a, 7b
HERE

A clear illustration of the periodic nature of the mode-locked solution is shown in phase space projections of the steady-state behavior of the system Figure 7b shows the phase portrait corresponding to the time-domain behavior in figure 7a Here, we have plotted simultaneous values of the capital sector capital K and the goods goods sector capital orders O_g over many cycles The horizontal axis represents the external forcing, and the vertical axis the response of the model Production capacity of the capital sector builds up and decays precisely once for each three swings of the external signal

Figure 8 shows the results obtained with the same amplitude of the forcing signal (A = 0 20), but with the forcing period T = 4 6 years This case, which could represent the interaction between the economic long wave and the short-term business cycle, produces 1 10 entrainment The long wave completes precisely one oscillation for each 10 business cycles The 1 10 mode-locked solution exists in the interval 4 47 ≤ T ≤ 4 70 years Near this interval we find intervals with entrainment ratios of 1 9, 1 11, 2 19, 2 21, etc

F1b 8a, 8b
HERE

To illustrate the variety of different behaviors that can result from relatively weak perturbations of the long wave model, figure 9 shows the results obtained with $A = 0\ 20$ and $T = 19\ 4$ years For the first 200 years, the model runs with a constant demand for capital to the goods sector, showing the undisturbed long wave oscillation In year 200, the external forcing begins After a short transient the model locks into a 2 6 solution, with 2 long waves for each 6 cycles of the external forcing This is a result of a period-doubling of the above 1 3 solution. The true period is now 116 4 years, and the half-period (which we may still identify as the long wave period) is 58 2 years

FIG 9
HERE

A more complete picture of the entrainment process is obtained by plotting the observed mode-locking ratio as a function of the forcing period Figure 10 shows an example of such a construction, a so-called devil's staircase (Mandelbrot 1977) The period of the external forcing has here been varied from 5 to 54 years while keeping the amplitude constant at $A = 0\ 025$ We observe a series of intervals with 1 n mode-locked solutions Between these, intervals with other commensurate winding numbers are observed In the region from $27 \leq T \leq 37$ years, for example, we find intervals with 3 5, 2 3, 3 4, 4 5 and 5 6 entrainment

FIG. 10
HERE

By refining the calculations one finds more and more resonances covering narrower and narrower intervals For small values of A the phenomenon has a self-similar structure that causes it to repeat ad infinitum on a smaller and smaller scale The fractal nature of the devil's staircase is illustrated in the insert of figure 10 Here, we have plotted some of the principal mode-locked solutions between the 1 3 and the 1 2 steps In practice, the finer details will be washed out by noise – the random shocks that continuously bombard the economy will not allow the trajectory to settle in the neighborhood of one of the more complicated solutions However, the more fundamental ratios, such as, for instance, 1 3 and 1 4 are stable over much broader intervals Mode locking can thus be robust to perturbations and noise that cause individual cycle shape and timing to vary

If the amplitude of the forcing signal is changed, the intervals of entrainment also change Figure 11 shows the principal mode-locked zones as a function of forcing period and amplitude For $A = $

0 there can, of course, be no entrainment at all   As A is increased, however, wider and wider intervals of mode-locked behavior develop, and the regions of mode locking, known as Arnol'd tongues, broaden   For small amplitudes quasiperiodic behavior exists between the tongues   The tongues cannot continue to grow, however. As the amplitude of the forcing signal grows the tongues begin to overlap, and quasiperiodic behavior then vanishes In our model this occurs at A $\approx 0\,025$ Above the critical value the trajectory is either periodic or chaotic

FIG 11
HERE

Figure 12 shows an example of chaotic behavior in the model. The period and amplitude of each long wave are now different. The period and the amplitude of the perturbing signal are T = 16 1 years and A = 0 20, respectively   Chaotic behavior is characterized by its sensitivity to initial conditions such that two simulations with initial conditions differing only slightly will diverge exponentially until the position of one bears no relation to that of the other

FIG. 12
HERE

A variety of complex nonlinear phenomena arise where the Arnol'd tongues overlap, including period doubling, intermittency, and frustration   Figure 13 shows a bifurcation diagram in which the 1 2 mode-locked solution is transformed into 2 4, 4:8, 8:16,   solutions as the forcing amplitude increases from 0 0475 to 0 0625 while maintaining T = 19.6 years   The variable plotted along the vertical axis in this diagram is the maximal production capital reached at the peak of each long wave   When the forcing amplitude is less than 0 048 all maxima are equal   For slightly higher amplitudes, however, the model bifurcates into a behavior where low and high maxima alternate. At about A = 0 0552 a new bifurcation occurs so that the model now shifts between 4 different maxima. The period-doubling cascade continues until at A $\approx$ 0.0570 the behavior becomes chaotic. As A is increased further we observe the characteristic windows of periodic behavior (Feigenbaum 1978) until finally, at about A = 0 0597, a sudden expansion of the chaotic attractor occurs. This represents a so-called crisis (Grebogi et al 1982), where the model now generates a complicated behavior in which intermittency chaos due to the interaction of the 1 3 solution with period-doubling chaos arising from the 1:2 solution

FIG 13
HERE

In other regions of the phase diagram, two or more periodic solutions coexist, and initial conditions (or subsequent perturbations) determine which solution the system chooses. This is, for instance, the case in the region around $T = 29.4$ years and $A = 0.05$, where the 2 3 and 3 5 tongues cross. Figure 14 shows a 200 x 200 point scan over the plane of initial conditions for the capital sector capital stock K and the capital sector supply line S. Black points indicate those initial conditions that lead to the 2 3 periodic solution, and white points indicate those conditions that lead to the 3 5 solution. The boundary between the basins of attraction for the two simultaneously existing periodic solutions is clearly fractal. Minor changes in initial conditions cause unpredictable, qualitative changes in the steady state behavior.

6 Conclusion

Recent developments in nonlinear dynamics, behavioral decision theory, and experimental economics have joined to form the basis for empirically testable, nonlinear, disequilibrium theories of economic dynamics grounded in experimental test and field study of economic decision making. The integration of these disciplines sheds significant light on the origin of aggregate cyclical movements at different frequencies, as well as the interaction of these modes. In particular, cyclical movements of different periodicities can arise through the interaction of boundedly rational decision making with the time delays, stock and flow structure, and nonlinearities fundamental to the structure of economic activity.

Behavioral models of disequilibrium dynamics show how firms can generate cycles that closely resemble the short term business cycle and the 15-25 year construction cycle. Incorporating positive feedback processes arising from macroeconomic couplings between firms and among the production, consumption, financial, and government sectors explains how the long wave can arise. Unlike the short term business cycle, the long wave appears to be a self-organized cycle that does not require continuous exogenous excitation to persist.

The approach described here also sheds light on the interaction of the different cyclical modes. The systematic coincidence of different cyclical modes in economic dynamics was suggested long ago by Schumpeter (1939), and Forrester (1977) proposed nonlinear entrainment as the explanation for the apparent mode-locking among macroeconomic cycles However, formal investigation of such macroeconomic entrainment processes with modern nonlinear theory does not appear to have been attempted before Though the model investigated here is highly simplified, we have shown how entrainment may arise in a system that captures basic macroeconomic feedback processes and fundamental nonlinearities such as nonnegativity and capacity constraints

More generally, entrainment can cause different oscillatory processes with approximately similar periods to move in phase at a single frequency, producing aggregate business fluctuations Nonlinear entrainment also accounts for the existence of a small number of relatively well-defined periodicities: oscillatory tendencies of similar periodicity in different parts of the economy are drawn together in 1 1 synchrony to form a single mode, and each of these modes is separated from the next by a wide enough margin to avoid entrainment at the same period Hence the economy exhibits clearly distinguishable modes economic historians have dubbed the business cycle, the Kuznets cycle, and the economic long wave, rather than fluctuations equally distributed at all frequencies and phases, fluctuations that would wash out in the aggregate

Even with relatively wide separation in periodicity, the interaction between modes may be strong enough to lock them together such that they have commensurate periods Nonlinear interactions may thus pull the Kuznets cycle and business cycle into phase with the long wave and accentuate its peaks or downturns Additionally, since mode-locking at a given rational winding number is stable over a finite range of individual cycle periods, mode-locking is robust with respect to variations in the parameters governing the individual cycles, allowing entrainment to persist over long time periods despite technological and institutional change, perturbations, and other sources of variation in economic life.

References

Arnol'd, V I 1965 Small Denominators I Mappings of the Circumference Onto Itself *Am Math Soc Translations* Ser 2, 46, 213-184

Arthur, B 1988 Self-reinforcing Mechanisms in Economics, in Anderson, P, K Arrow, & D Pines (eds), *The Economy as an Evolving Complex System,* Reading, MA Addison-Wesley

Bakken, B 1992 Learning and Transfer of Understanding Dynamic Decision Environments PhD Dissertation Sloan School of Management, MIT, Cambridge MA 02139

Bieshaar, H and A Kleinknecht 1984 Kondratiev Long Waves in Aggregate Output? An Econometric Test, *Konjunkturpolitik* 30, 279 - 303

Brehmer, B 1990 Strategies in real-time, dynamic decision making, in R Hogarth (ed), *Insights in Decision Making,* Chicago University of Chicago Press, 262-279

Brøns, M. and J Sturis 1991 Local and Global Bifurcations in a Model of the Economic Long Wave, *System Dynamics Review* 7, 41-60

Burns, A 1969 *The Business Cycle in a Changing World* New York National Bureau of Economic Research

Colding-Jorgensen, M 1983 A Model for the Firing Pattern of a Paced Nerve Cell, *Journal of Theoretical Biology* 101, 541 - 568

Day, R , 1982 Irregular Growth Cycles, *American Economic Review,* 72, 406-414

Diehl, E 1992 Effects of Feedback Structure on Dynamic Decision Making, PhD dissertation, Sloan School of Management, MIT, Cambridge MA 02139

Dosi, G , et al 1988 Technical Change and Economic Theory London Pinter

van Duijn, J J 1983 *The Long Wave in Economic Life,* George Allen and Unwin, London

Feigenbaum, M. 1978 Quantitative universality for a class of nonlinear transformations *Journal of Statistical Physics* 19, 25-52 and 21, 669-706

Fisher, I 1933 The Debt-Deflation Theory of Great Depressions, *Econometrica,* 1, 337-57

Forrester, J W. 1987 Nonlinearity in High-Order Models of Social Systems, *European Journal of Operational Research,* 30, 104-109

Forrester, J 1981 Innovation and Economic Change. *Futures*. 13, 323-331.

Forrester, J W 1979 An Alternative Approach to Economic Policy Macrobehavior from Microstructure In Kamrany, N. and R Day (eds), *Economic Issues of the Eighties* Baltimore Johns Hopkins University Press.

Forrester J W 1977 Growth Cycles, *De Economist* 125, 525 - 543

Forrester, J. 1976. Business Structure, Economic Cycles, and National Policy *Futures* 8, 195-214

Forrester, J W , 1961 *Industrial Dynamics* Cambridge MIT Press

Forrester, N 1982. A dynamic synthesis of basic macroeconomic theory· implications for stabilization policy analysis PhD dissertation, Sloan School of Management, MIT, Cambridge MA 02139.

Freeman, C (ed.) 1982 Long Waves in the World Economy London Butterworth

Freeman, C , J Clark, L Soete, 1982 *Unemployment and Technical Innovation A Study of Long Waves and Economic Development* Westport, CT: Greenwood Press

Frisch, R 1933 Propagation Problems and Impulse Problems in Dynamic Economics In Gordon, R and L Klein (eds), *Readings in Business Cycles* Homewood, IL Richard D Irwin (1965)

Garvy, G 1943 Kondratieff's Theory of Long Cycles *Review of Economic Statistics* 25(4), 203-220

Glass, L A. Shrier, and J Belair 1986. Chaotic Cardiac Rhythms, in *Chaos*, ed A V Holden, Nonlinear Science Theory and Applications, Manchester University Press, England

Glass, L, M. Guevara, J Belair, and A Shrier 1984. Global Bifurcations in a Periodically Forced Biological Oscillator *Physical Review A* 29, 1348-1357.

Glazier, J., M Jensen, A. Libchaber, & J Stavans 1986 Structure of Arnold tongues and the $f(a)$ spectrum for period doubling: experimental results, *Physical Review A*, 34(2), 1621-1624

Goldstein, J. 1988. *Long Cycles Prosperity and War in the Modern Age*. New Haven Yale University Press

Goodwin, R , 1951 The nonlinear accelerator and the persistence of business cycles, *Econometrica*, 19, 1-17

Gordon, Robert A 1951 *Business Fluctuations*, Harper and Row, New York

Graham, A and P. Senge, 1980 A Long Wave Hypothesis of Innovation, *Technological Forecasting and Social Change*, 17, 283-311

Grebogi, C , E Ott, and J Yorke 1982 Chaotic Attractors in Crisis *Physical Review Letters* 48, 1507-1510

Hogarth, R , 1987 *Judgement and Choice 2nd Edition* Chichester John Wiley

Homer, J 1980 The Role of Consumer Demand in Business Cycle Entrainment Working paper D-3227-1, System Dynamics Group, MIT E40-294, Cambridge MA 02139

Hoyt, H 1933 *One Hundred Years of Land Values in Chicago,* University of Chicago Press, Chicago

Jensen, M H , P Bak, & T Bohr 1983 Complete Devil's Staircase, Fractal Dimension, and Universality of Mode-Locking Structure in the Circle Map, *Physical Review Letters* 50, 1637-1639

Jensen, M H , P. Bak, and T Bohr 1984 Transition to Chaos by Interaction of Resonances in Dissipative Systems I Circle Maps, *Physical Review A* 30, 1960 - 1969

Kahneman, D , P Slovic, and A Tversky, 1982 *Judgment Under Uncertainty Heuristics and Biases,* Cambridge Cambridge University Press

Kaldor, N 1940 A Model of the Trade Cycle *Economic Journal* 50, 78-92

Kampmann, C 1984 Disaggregating a Simple Model of the Economic Long Wave. System Dynamics Group Working Paper D-3641, Sloan School of Management, MIT, Cambridge MA 02139

Kampmann, C , & Sterman, J D 1992 Do Markets Mitigate Misperceptions of Feedback in Dynamic Tasks? Working Paper 3421-92-BPS, May, Sloan School of Management, MIT, Cambridge, MA 02139

Kleinknecht, A 1984 Prosperity, Crises, and Innovation Patterns, *Cambridge Journal of Economics* 8(3)

Kondratiev, N D 1935 The Long Waves in Economic Life, *Review of Economic Statistics* 17, 105 - 115

Kondratiev, N. D 1928/1984. *The Long Wave Cycle* G Daniels (tr). New York: Richardson and Snyder.

Kuznets, S. 1973 Modern Economic Growth Findings and Reflections, *American Economic Review* 63, 247 - 258.

Long, C D. Jr. 1940 *Building Cycles and the Theory of Investment*, Princeton University Press, New Jersey

Lorenz, H-W 1989 *Nonlinear Dynamical Economics and Chaotic Motion* Berlin Springer Verlag

Low, G , 1980 The multiplier-accelerator model of business cycles interpreted from a system dynamics perspective, in J. Randers (ed), *Elements of the System Dynamics Method*, MIT Press, Cambridge

Mandel, E 1980 *Long Waves of Capitalist Development* Cambridge· Cambridge University Press

Mandelbrot, B B 1977 *Fractals Form, Change and Dimension*, Freeman, San Francisco

Mansfield, E 1983 Long Waves and Technological Innovation *American Economic Association, Papers and Proceedings*,73(2), 141-145.

Mass, N 1975 *Economic Cycles An Analysis of Underlying Causes* MIT Press/Productivity Press

Meadows, D H., D L. Meadows, J Randers 1992 *Beyond the Limits* Post Mills, VT Chelsea Green Publishing Co

Mensch, G 1979 *Stalemate in Technology* Cambridge, MA Ballinger

Metzler, L 1941 The nature and stability of inventory cycles *Review of Economic Statistics* 23, 113-129

Mitchell, T 1923 Competitive illusion as a cause of business cycles *Quarterly Journal of Economics* 38, 631-652

Mitchell, W C. 1927 *Business Cycles The Problem and Its Setting*, National Bureau of
Economic Research, New York

Montaño, M and W Ebeling 1980 A Stochastic Evolutionary Model of Technological Change,
Collective Phenomena 3, 107-114

Moore, H G (ed) 1961 *Business Cycle Indicators*, National Bureau of Economic Research,
Princeton University Press, New Jersey

Morecroft, J 1985 Rationality in the analysis of behavioral simulation models, *Management
Science* 31(7), 900-916

Mosekilde, E and S Rasmussen 1986 Technical Economic Succession and the Economic Long
Wave *European Journal of Operational Research* 25, 27-38

Mosekilde, E , R Feldberg, C Knudsen, and M Hindsholm 1990 Mode Locking and
Spatiotemporal Chaos in Periodically Driven Gunn Diodes *Physical Review B* 41, 2298-
2306

Mosekilde, E , Larsen, E R , Sterman, J D , & Thomsen, J S 1992 Nonlinear Mode-
Interaction in the Macroeconomy *Annals of Operations Research*, 37, 185-215

Paich, M , & Sterman, J D 1992 Boom, Bust, and Failures to Learn in Experimental Markets
Working Paper 3441-92 BPS, July, Sloan School of Management, Cambridge, MA 02139

Rand, D, S Ostlund, J Sethna, and E Siggia 1982 Universal Transition from Quasiperiodicity
to Chaos in Dissipative Systems. *Physical Review Letters* 49, 132-135

Randers, J , 1984 The Tanker Market, Working Paper 84/9, Norwegian School of Management,
Oslo

Rasmussen, S , E Mosekilde, and J Holst 1989 Empirical indication of economic long waves in
aggregate production, *European Journal of Operational Research*, 42, 279-293.

Rasmussen, S , E Mosekilde, and J D Sterman 1985 Bifurcations and Chaotic Behavior in a
Simple Model of the Economic Long Wave, *System Dynamics Review* 1, 92 - 110

Riggleman, J R 1933 Building Cycles in the United States, 1897 - 1932, *Journal of the
American Statistical Association* 28, 182

Rosenberg, N and C Frischtak 1983 Long Waves and Economic Growth A Critical

Appraisal *American Economic Association, Papers and Proceedings,*73(2), 146-151

Rostow, W W 1978 *The World Economy History and Prospect*, MacMillan Press, London

Samuelson, P A , 1939 Interactions between the multiplier analysis and the principle of acceleration, *The Review of Economic Statistics,* 21, 75-78

Samuelson, P A 1947 *Foundations of Economic Analysis* Cambridge. Harvard University Press

Schumpeter, J A 1939 *Business Cycles*, New York: McGraw-Hill Book Company

Semmler, W (ed) 1989 *Financial Dynamics and Business Cycles New Perspectives* Armonk, NY M E Sharpe

Senge, P 1980 A System Dynamics Approach to Investment Function Formulation and Testing, *Socioeconomic Planning Sciences,* 14, 269-80

Silverberg, G 1988 Modeling Economic Dynamics and Technical Change Mathematical Approach to Self-Organization and Evolution, in Dosi et al (eds), *Technical Change and Economic Theory* London Pinter

Simon, H 1979 Rational Decisionmaking in Business Organizations, *American Economic Review,* 69, 493-513

Simon , H , 1982 *Models of Bounded Rationality,* The MIT Press, Cambridge

Smith, V , Suchanek, G , and A Williams 1988 Bubbles, Crashes, and Endogenous Expectations in Experimental Spot Asset Markets, *Econometrica,* 56(5), 1119-1152

Sterman, J D 1992 Long Wave Decline and the Politics of Depression *Bank Credit Analyst* 44, 26-42. Revised and extended version available from author.

Sterman, J. D 1990 A Long Wave Perspective on the Economy in the 1990s *Bank Credit Analyst.* 42, 28-47

Sterman, J D 1989a Misperceptions of feedback in dynamic decision making, *Organizational Behavior and Human Decision Processes* 43(3), 301-335

Sterman, J D. 1989b Modeling managerial behavior misperceptions of feedback in a dynamic decision making experiment, *Management Science* 35(3), 321-339

Sterman, J D 1989c Deterministic Chaos in an Experimental Economic System *Journal of Economic Behavior and Organization*, 12, 1-28

Sterman, J D 1988 Nonlinear Dynamics in the World Economy The Economic Long Wave In Christiansen, P & Parmentier, **R** (Eds), *Structure, Coherence, and Chaos in Dynamical Systems* Manchester Manchester University Press, 389-413

Sterman, J D 1987 Testing Behavioral Simulation Models by Direct Experiment *Management Science*, 33(12), 1572-1592

Sterman, J D 1986a The Economic Long Wave Theory and Evidence, *System Dynamics Review*, 2(2), 87-125

Sterman, J D 1986b Debt, Default, and Long Waves Is History Relevant? *Bank Credit Analyst*, *38*(5), 28-42

Sterman, J D 1985 A Behavioral Model of the Economic Long Wave, *Journal of Economic Behavior and Organization*, 6(2), 17-53

Szymkat and Mosekilde 1986 Global Bifurcation Analysis of An Economic Long Wave Model *Proc 2nd European Simulation Conference*, Antwerp, Belgium San Diego Simulation Council, Inc , 139-145

Togeby, M , E Mosekilde, and J. Sturis 1988 Frequency-Locking in a Model of Two Coupled Thermostatically Controlled Radiators, *Proc Winter Annual Meeting of the American Society of Mechanical Engineers*, paper 88-WA/DSC - 14

Vasko, T (ed) 1987 *The Long Wave Debate* Berlin Springer Verlag/IIASA

Wolf, A 1986 Quantifying Chaos with Lyapunov Exponents, in A V Holden (ed) *Chaos* Manchester Manchester University Press

Zannetos, Z 1966 The Theory of Oil Tankship Rates Cambridge, MA. The MIT Press

Zarnowitz, V 1985 Recent Work on Business Cycles in Historical Perspective A Review of Theories and Evidence, *Journal of Economic Literature* 23, 523-80

Figure captions

Figure 1   US Industrial Production and civilian unemployment rate, 1947-1992   The evolution of the system reflects the interaction of multiple modes of behavior long-term growth, business cycles, and the long wave (production and unemployment grow on average and fluctuate with the short-term business cycle   The long wave causes the rise in the average level of unemployment and the slowdown in economic growth since about 1970, this is more easily seen in the detrended data (figures 2 and 4)

Figure 2   Detrended US industrial production at three levels of the distribution chain, showing the characteristic amplification of business cycle fluctuations from production of consumer goods through intermediate goods to raw materials   Note also the phase lag as the cycle propagates from consumer goods production to raw materials   The long-term trend of $\approx$ 29%/month has been removed to highlight the business cycle

Figure 3   The real-estate or construction cycle, illustrated here by the vacancy rate for commercial office space in downtown Boston, 1952 - 1990 (see also figure 6)   Source Bakken 1992

Figure 4   US real GNP, detrended by removing the long-term average exponential growth rate since 1800   The deviations from the long-term trend reflect the interactions of the cyclical modes, particularly the business cycle and long wave (and noise)   The long wave causes growth to be faster than trend from 1947 through about 1970, and slower than trend since   Note the large amplitude of the long wave compared to the business cycle. During the long-wave expansion business cycle recessions seem to be short and mild, during the long-wave decline recessions appear to be longer and deeper

Figure 5   Limit cycle behavior of the simple long wave model   The steady state behavior is shown   There are no exogenous sources of variation

Figure 6. (a) Oil tanker spot rates (worldscale units; 100 = normal profitability); (b) Capacity utilization of the world tanker fleet, showing nonlinear interaction of the short-term business cycle in demand for oil transport with the endogenous 20 year construction cycle in tanker supply   Source Bakken (1992)

Figure 7   (a) Time domain and and (b) phase space behavior of long wave model with 22 2 year exogenous forcing in demand for capital from the goods sector   The period of the long wave adjusts to maintain 1 3 entrainment with the exogenous fluctuation

Figure 8   (a) Time domain and (b) phase space behavior of long wave model with 4 6 year forcing in demand for capital from the goods sector   Now the period of the long wave adjusts to maintain 1 10 entrainment with the forcing fluctuation

Figure 9   In year 200 the demand for capital of the goods sector begins to fluctuation with amplitude 20 and period 19 4 years   The system quickly entrains with a 2 6 solution

Figure 10   Devil's Staircase, showing dependence of mode-locking ratio on the frequency of the forcing function   Mode locking exists at every rational winding number and is stable over a finite interval of the forcing frequency   The staircase is a self-similar fractal as shown in the inset

Figure 11   Arnol'd diagram showing dependence of the intervals of mode-locking on the amplitude of the forcing function   The so-called Arnol'd tongues of mode-locked solutions increase in width as the amplitude of the forcing signal increases, until they begin to overlap at the critical line

Figure 12   Chaotic behavior of the model with A = 20 and T = 16 1 years

Figure 13   Bifurcation diagram showing maximum capital stock in each long wave as a function of the forcing amplitude A   As the amplitude of the forcing signal, and thus the coupling between the endogenous and exogenous cycles, grows, the model experiences a period doubling cascade to chaos

Figure 14   200 x 200 point scan over the plane of initial conditions for the capital sector capital stock K and the capital sector supply line S, normalized so base case values = 1 0   Black points indicate steady-state entrainment with a 2 3 ratio, white points indicate 3 5 entrainment   The basin boundary is fractal   Here A = 05 and T = 29 4 years

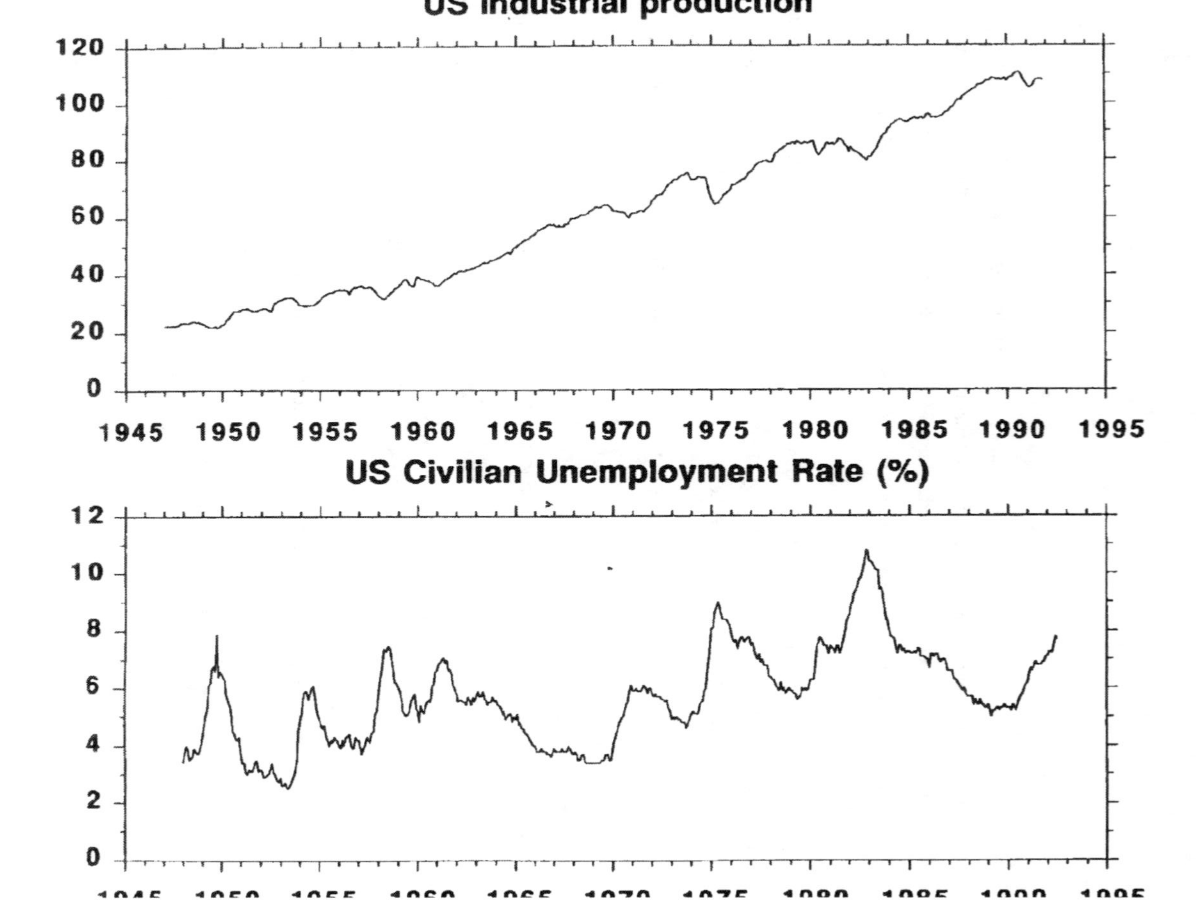

US Industrial production
120
100
80
60
40
20
0
1945 1950 1955 1960 1965 1970 1975 1980 1985 1990 1995
US Civilian Unemployment Rate (%)
12
10
8
6
4
2
0
1945 1950 1955 1960 1965 1970 1975 1980 1985 1990 1995

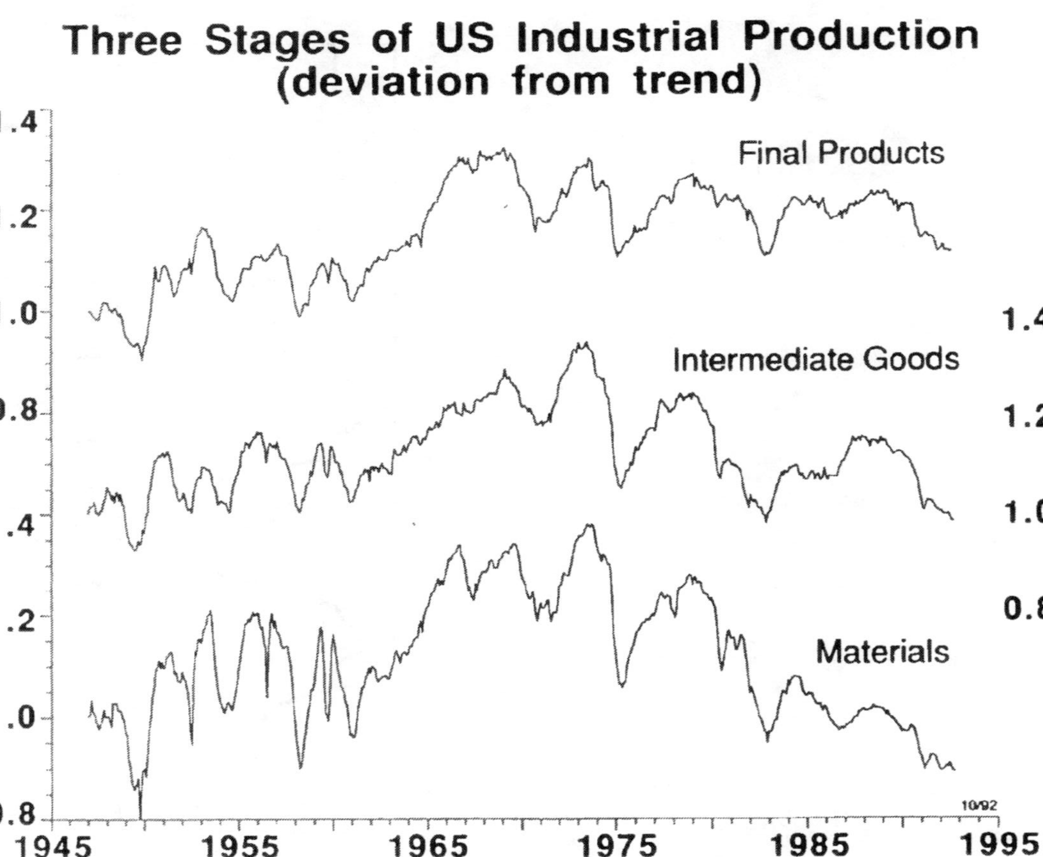

Three Stages of US Industrial Production
(deviation from trend)
Final Products
Intermediate Goods
Materials
1.4
1.2
1.0
0.8
1.4
1.2
1.0
0.8
1.4
1.2
1.0
0.8
1945
1955
1965
1975
1985
1995
10/92

Commercial vacancy rate,
Downtown Boston (%)
18
12
6
0
52 56 60 64 68 72 76 80 84 88

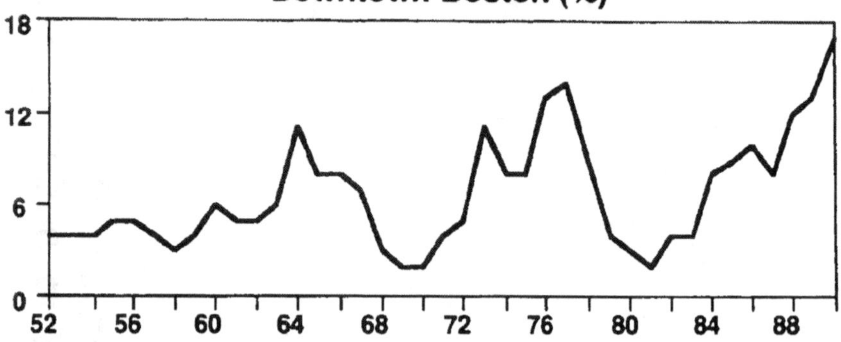

Figure 3

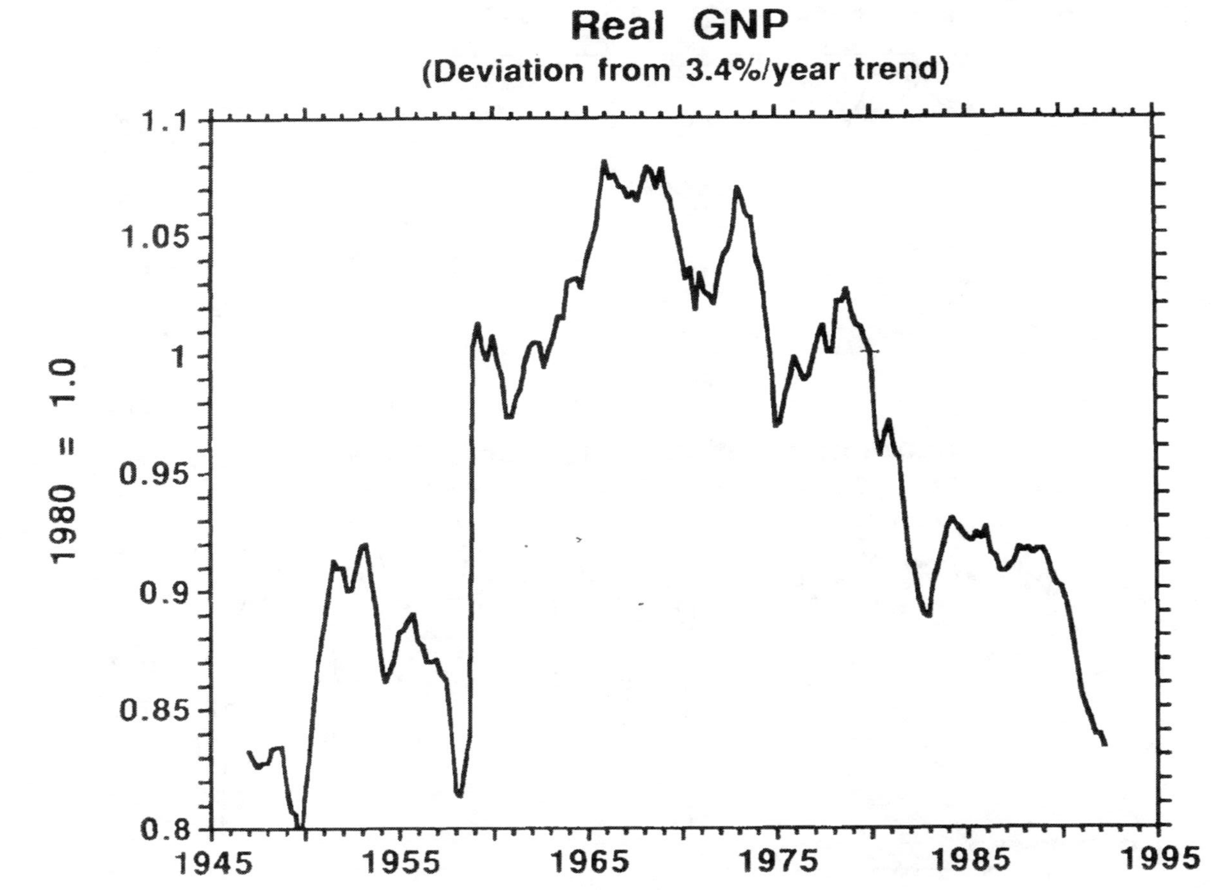

Real GNP
(Deviation from 3.4%/year trend)
1980 = 1.0
1.1
1.05
1
0.95
0.9
0.85
0.8
1945
1955
1965
1975
1985
1995

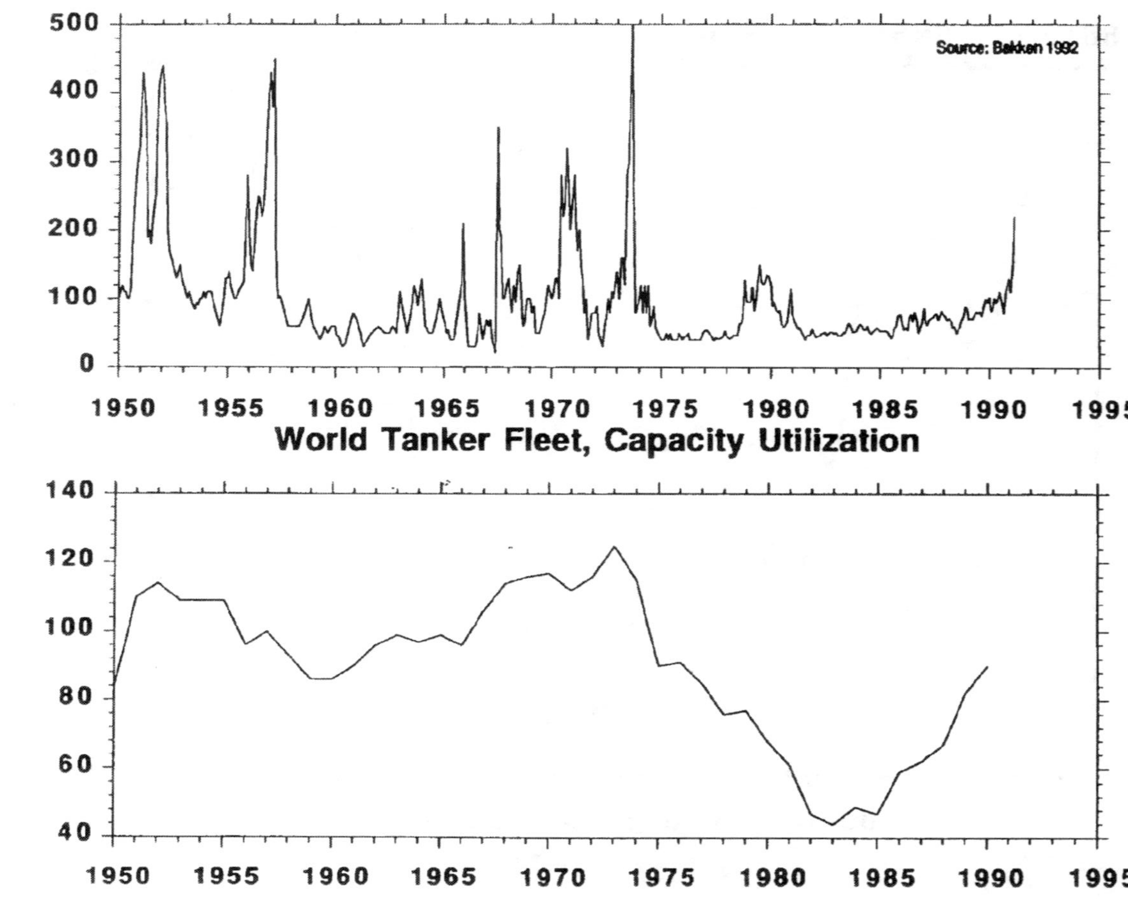

Source: Bakken 1992
World Tanker Fleet, Capacity Utilization

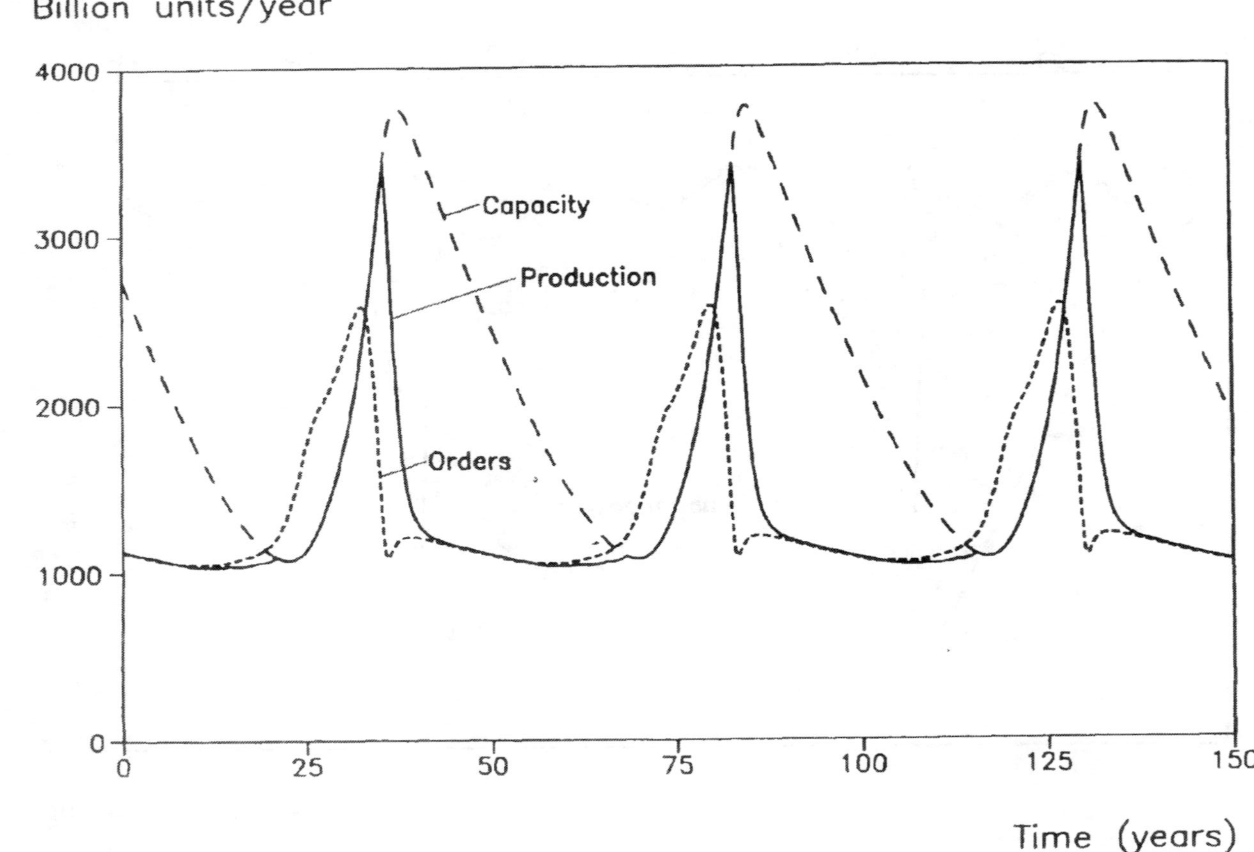

Billion units/year
4000
3000
2000
1000
0
Capacity
Production
Orders
0
25
50
75
100
125
150
Time (years)

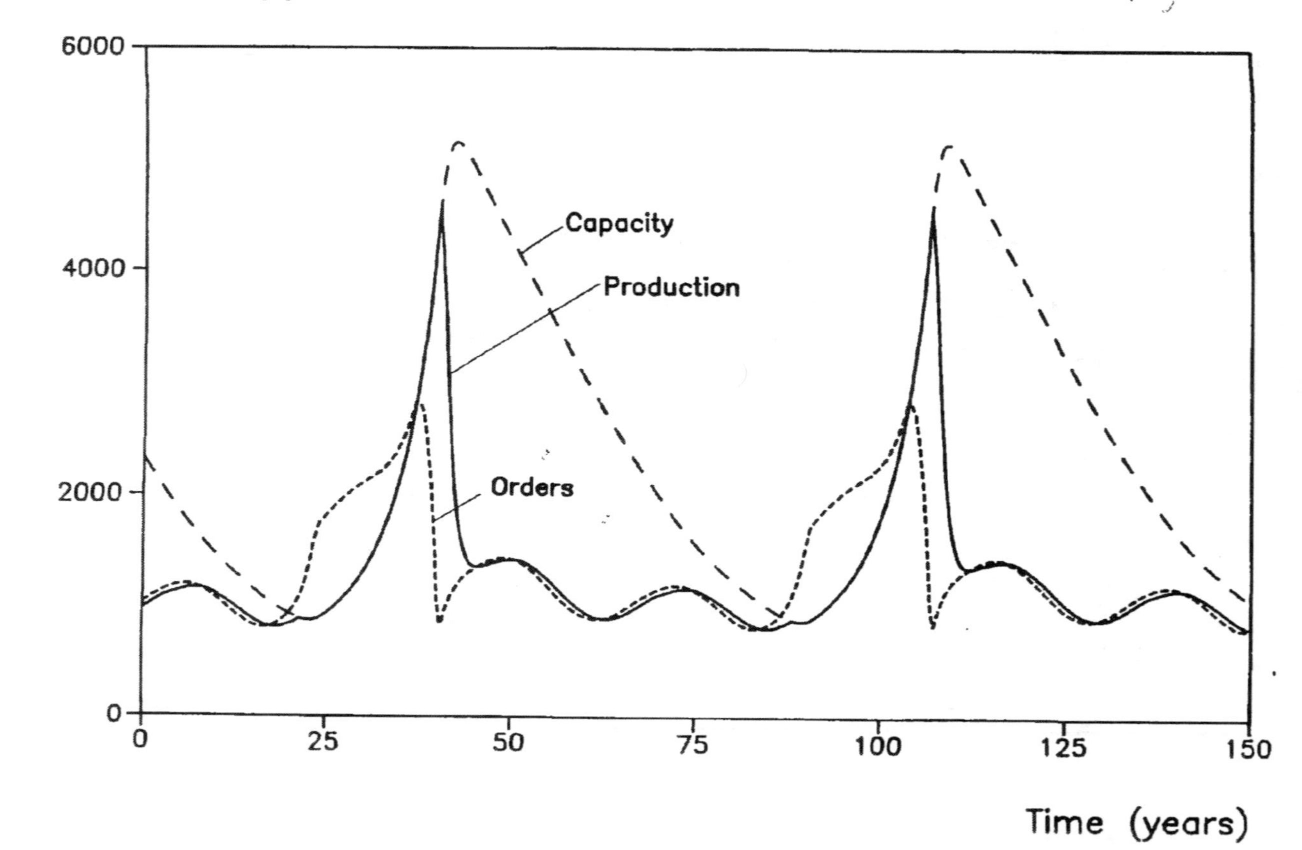

Billion units/year
6000
4000
2000
0
Capacity
Production
Orders
0
25
50
75
100
125
150
Time (years)
Figure 7a

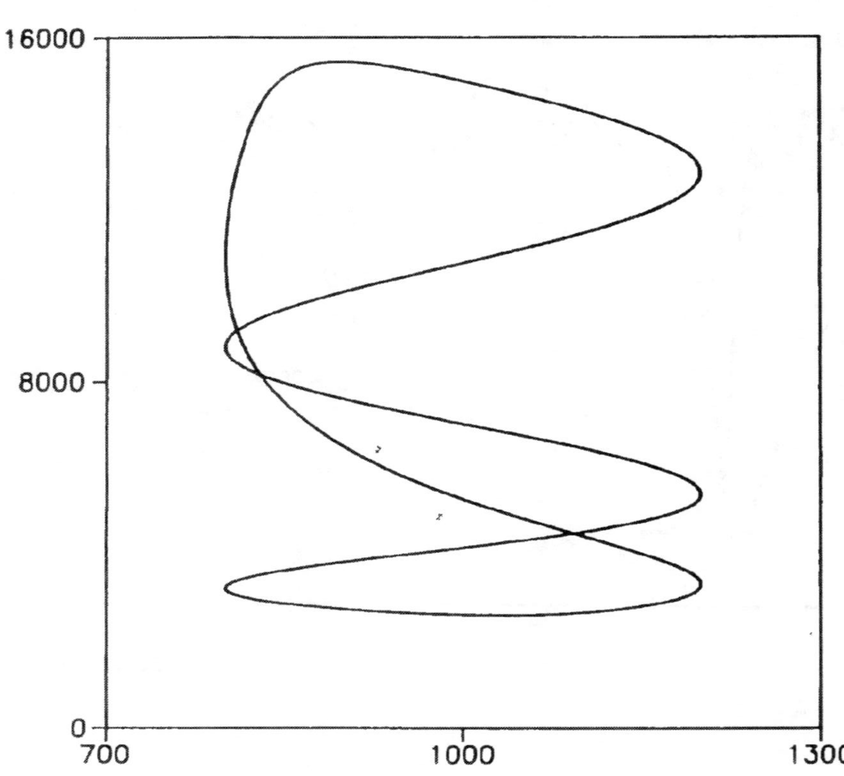

Figure 76

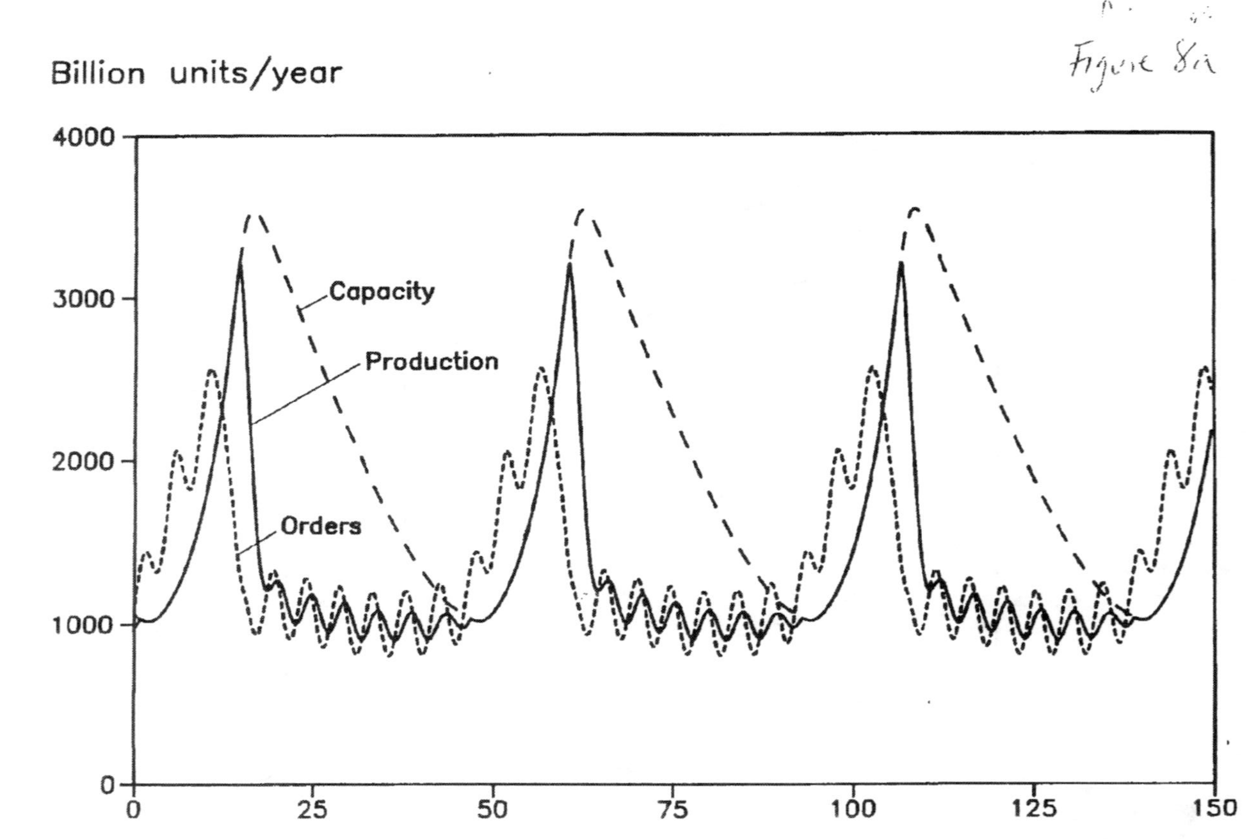

Billion units/year
4000
3000
2000
1000
0
Capacity
Production
Orders
0
25
50
75
100
125
150
Figure 8a

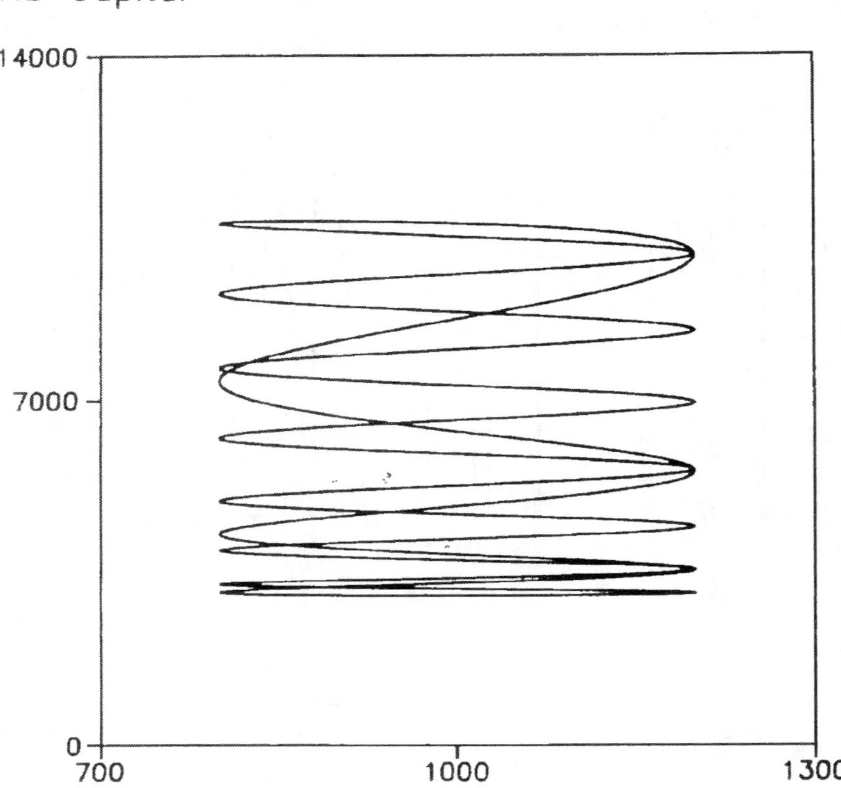

Figure 8b

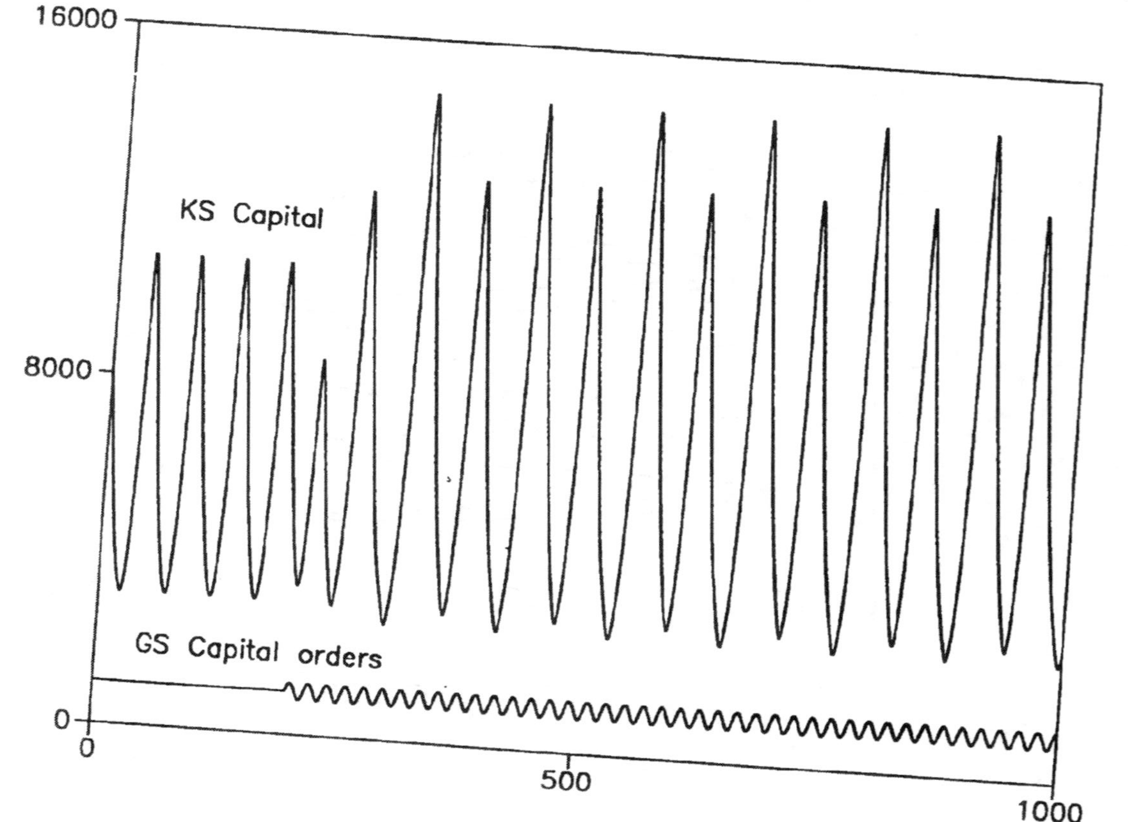

Figure 9

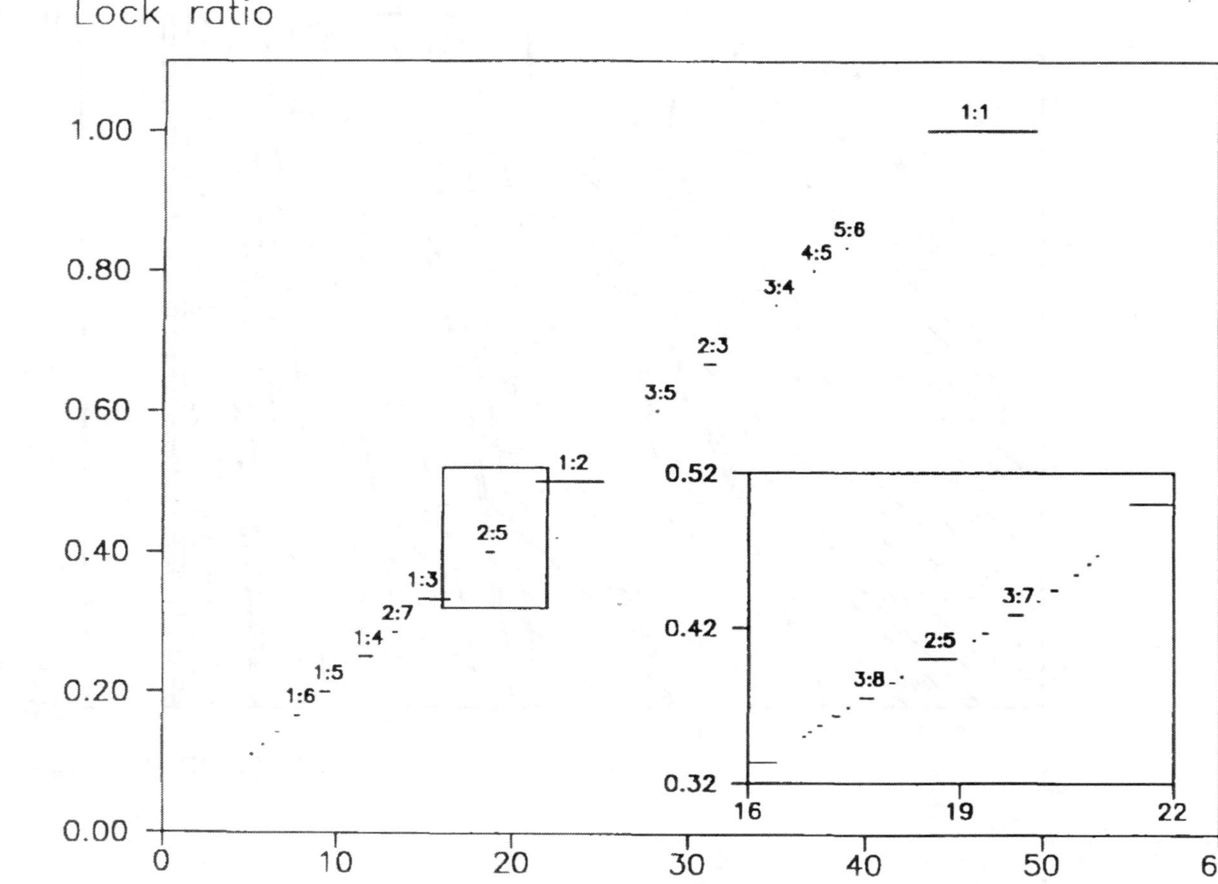

Lock ratio
1.00
0.80
0.60
0.40
0.20
0.00
0
10
20
30
40
50
60
1:1
5:6
4:5
3:4
2:3
3:5
1:2
2:5
1:3
2:7
1:4
1:5
1:6
0.52
0.42
0.32
16
19
22
3:7
2:5
3:8

Forcing amplitude
0.0
0.1
0.2
0
20
40
60
1:4
1:3
2:6
4:12
2:5
1:2
2:4
4:8
3:5
3:4
2:3
4:5
1:1
2:2
4:4

Figure 11

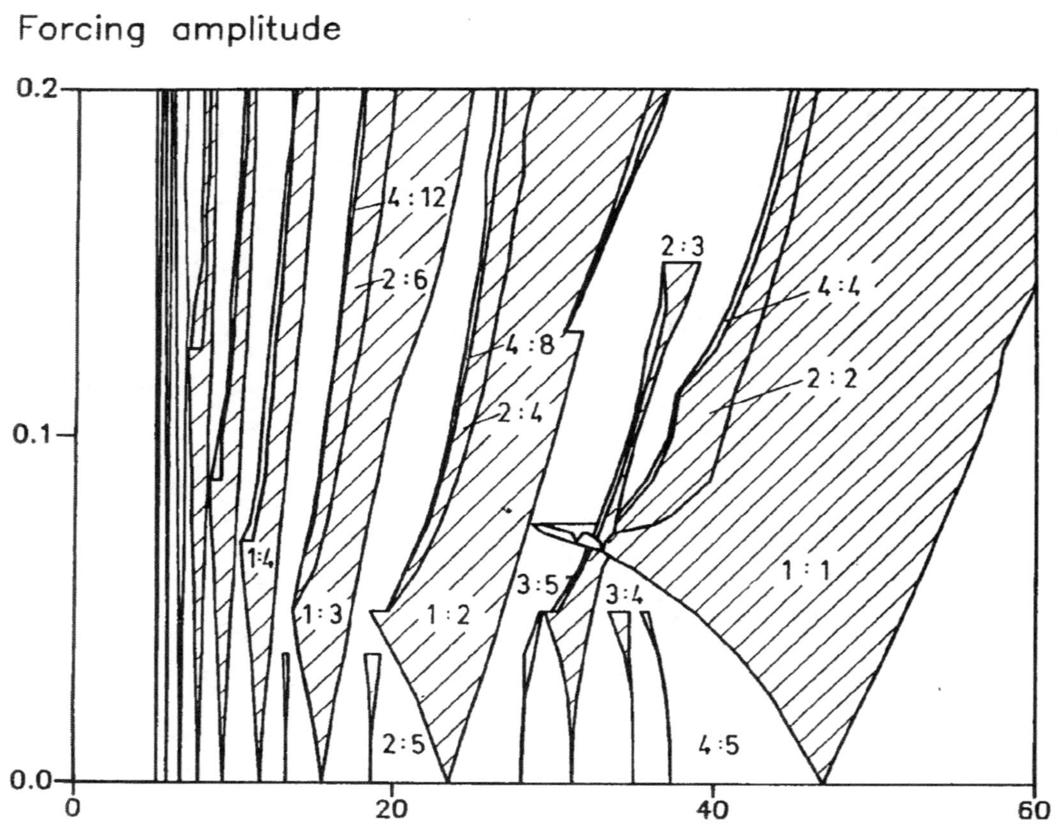

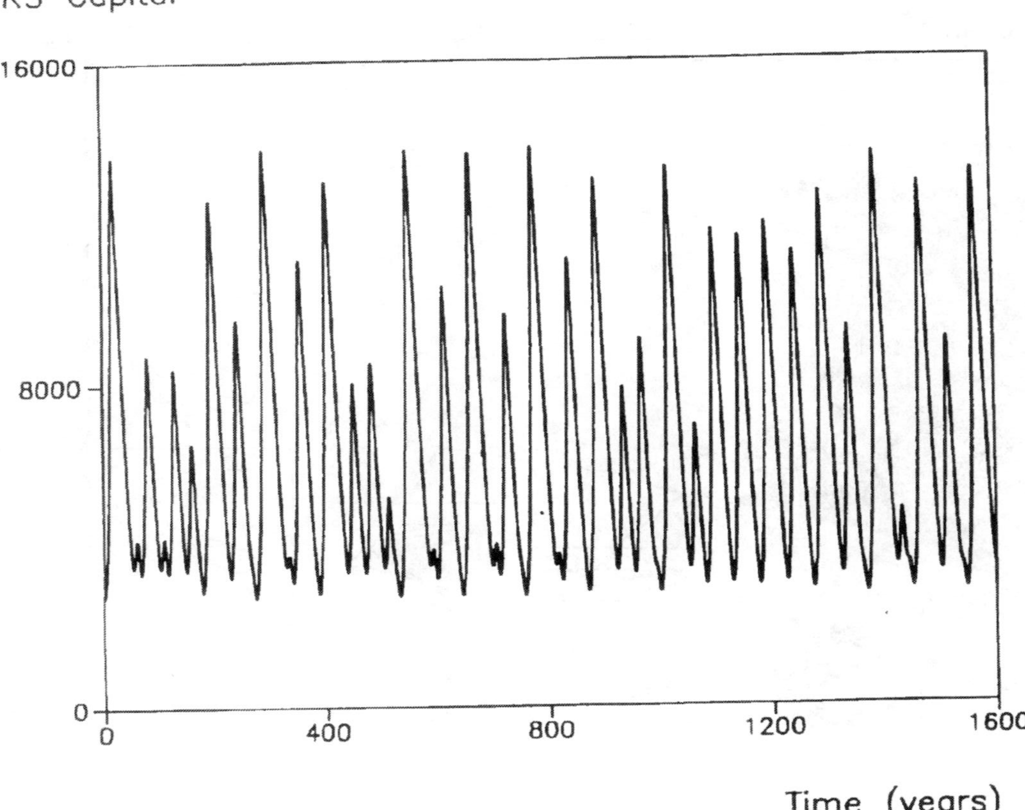

Figure 12

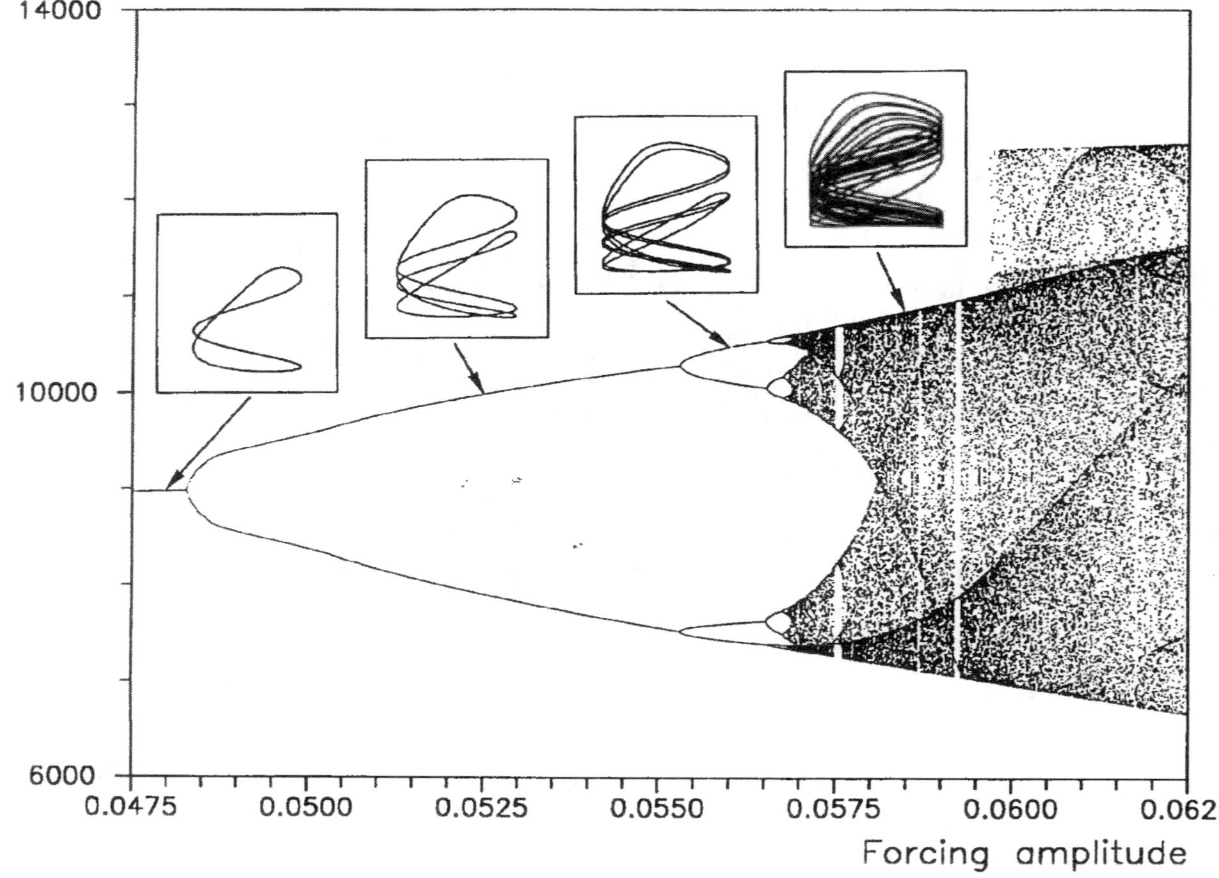

14000
10000
6000
0.0475
0.0500
0.0525
0.0550
0.0575
0.0600
0.0625
Forcing amplitude

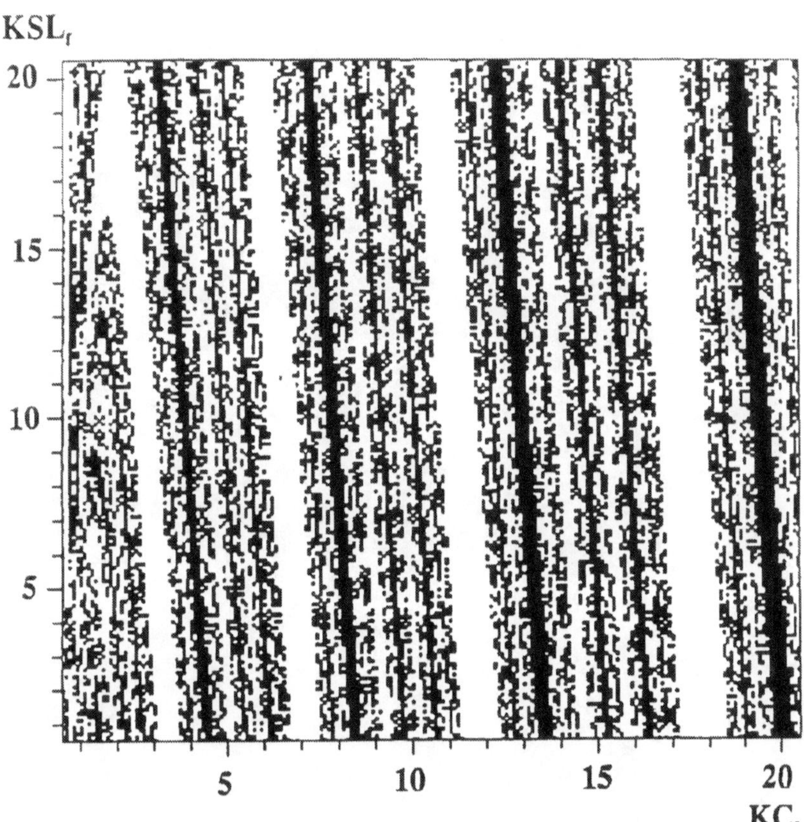

Figure 14